the
ELUSIVENESS OF
EQUALITY

the ELUSIVENESS OF EQUALITY

ALEXANDRA MCGROARTY

atmosphere press

*A heartful thank you to: Nydia Han, Justine Lindsay,
Magali Roy, and Nicole Ryan for allowing me to tell
their stories in relation to furthering diversity, equity and
inclusion in their respective fields.*

TABLE OF CONTENTS

CHAPTER ONE – RECAPPING WOMEN'S EQUITY IN THE 21ST CENTURY ... 1

Moving Past Science Fiction and Comedy ... 2

What *Bridging the Gap* Covered ... 4

Moving Our Mindsets ... 14

CHAPTER TWO – THE IDENTITY INDEX ... 17

Conclusion ... 27

CHAPTER THREE – LEARNING AND UNLEARNING GENDER ROLES ... 28

The Basics, Beginning with Childhood ... 30

The Basics, Continuing with Language ... 33

Conclusion ... 39

CHAPTER FOUR – MEDIA IN THE DEI REVOLUTION ... 40

The Power of Representation ... 40

The People We Watch ... 42

The Stories We Love ... 45

When Does It Go Wrong? ... 48

Conclusion ... 49

CHAPTER FIVE – REAL HOUSEWIVES AND BEYOND ... 51

Portrayal of Women in the Media ... 51

Un-Reality ... 53

Media Analysis and Interventions ... 55

A Woman's Voice: Nicole Ryan ... 57

The Glass Ceiling, the Glass Booth, and the Glass Desk ... 60

The Power of Media to Drive Change ... 63

Using Her Voice for Change: Nydia Han ... 64

Conclusion ... 66

CHAPTER SIX - SPORTS AND GENDER 68
Universal Inclusion: Magali Roy 69
Going Back: Women's Inclusion in Sports 70
Controversy Surrounding Transgender Athletes 74
Debunking Myths about Transgender Athletes 76
Windmills 78
The Importance of Inclusive Policies and Practices 78
Men's Sports, Women's Sports, and the Nonbinary 81
The Growing Backlash and Recent Legislation 82
Conclusion 84

CHAPTER SEVEN - JUSTINE LINDSAY,
A TRAILBLAZING CHEERLEADER 85

CHAPTER EIGHT - TOUCHDOWN FOR EQUITY 90
Jalen Hurts' All-Female Management Team 90

CHAPTER NINE - NON-BINARY AND THIRD GENDER
RECOGNITION AND THE LAW 94
Legal Challenges and Human Rights Advocacy 95
Depathologizing Trans Identities 97
The Fallout of Inequity in the United States 98
Understanding Power and Intersectionality 100
What Citizens Can Do: Advocacy and Activism 102
Legal Gender Recognition: A Distant Dream? 103

CHAPTER TEN - KNOW THE LGBTQ+ MOVEMENT 105
LGBTQ+ Timeline 106
Two Steps Back: Trump's Record of Action Against
Transgender People 114
Conclusion 116

CHAPTER ELEVEN - BEING AN ALLY 118
What Issues Does the LGBTQ+ Community Face? 119
What Does It Mean to Be an "Ally"? 120

Steps Toward Allyship   121

Promoting Inclusivity in the Workplace   125

Supporting Change as It Happens   127

Conclusion   130

CHAPTER TWELVE – FROM ALLYSHIP TO ACTIVISM   131

Taking Action: How You Can Get Involved   131

Amplifying LGBTQ+ Voices   133

LGBTQ+ Resources and Assistance   134

Activism for Women's Rights   136

Activism in the Right-to-Choose Movement   138

Understanding the Right-to-Choose Movement   142

Conclusion   144

CHAPTER THIRTEEN – ELUSIVE EQUITY   145

Recent Setbacks   145

What Can Be Done   148

Looking Towards Equity   149

♥

CHAPTER ONE: RECAPPING WOMEN'S EQUITY IN THE 21ST CENTURY

In 2022 I published my book *Bridging the Gap*, in which I discussed the state of gender equity in the 21st-century workplace. I'm proud of that book because while I focused on women's inequity compared to men in the workplace, I ultimately promoted equity across the board, encouraging us to accept each other's authenticity. People allowed to be their authentic selves are happier and more productive.

Nevertheless, the book did focus on workplace equity for women because, even now, much of the gestalt of the United States workforce – environments, rewards systems, leadership ideals, teamwork approaches, and day-to-day functions – is judged by a **masculine, Eurocentric, and heteronormative** standard.

The workforce was built this way and reinforced for decades. Now whenever women, or other marginalized groups, wedge themselves into that pre-ordained shape, they are automatically at a disadvantage. The archetypal workplace was not designed for diversity. Most people often conform to this bias without noticing; it's a deep, systemic problem that must be dragged out into the light kicking and screaming before someone says, "Oh heck, I hadn't even thought about that. We *do* have a problem!"

Bridging the Gap was mainly about the biases and inequities suffered by women because that inequity affects the most people, and I said as much. From that point, inequity worsens when a person presents with additional diversity. The more "different" one is from our idealized Eurocentric, masculine, heteronormative standard of "a great employee," or in fact, just a "normal person," the more problems of equity arise. Add race into the mix, and people are further marginalized. A Black woman suffers more inequity than a white woman. Add sexual orientation, and things get even worse. A gay Black woman is at three intersections of injustice.

But much of our consideration of gender equity has a dividing line, the assumption that we're dealing with two genders: men and women. What happens when we understand that humans might also be both genders or neither? Well, that's undoubtedly not heteronormative. It's a different level of differentness, and many of us are feeling our way along, adapting to this new landscape.

Oh, it's not new to humanity. But it is relatively new for us to talk about it.

MOVING PAST SCIENCE FICTION AND COMEDY

In Chapter Two, I'll define terms that our language recognizes today so that when we discuss the variety of humanity, we'll all be on the same page. Let's establish that "sex" and "gender" mean different things. "Sex" is a biological term connected with organs, chromosomes, and hormones. "Gender" describes the standards and norms society applies to someone of a particular sex.

In large part, our society has long assumed that someone's sex automatically implies their gender. Therein lies what I see as the crux of most of our misunderstanding: sex does not automatically imply gender, and we forget that – or dismiss it.

Before the turn of the 21st century, most of us were raised thinking there were two sexes – male and female. There were two genders – man and woman. But we weren't living under a rock: we knew about sex-change operations, about being gay or bisexual, and that sometimes people like to dress as the opposite gender. By and large, though, everything we thought was based on two genders. The notion of an "opposite" gender means there are just two, right? This was taken as fact, something so obvious that upending it was a matter for science fiction and comedy.

Star Trek: The Next Generation made an episode about a planet whose denizens had only one sex – weird! – though its purpose was to mirror the homophobia of the era. The character who declared a gender openly, saying "I am female," was ultimately "fixed" by nefarious medical means. *Farscape* included a bit in which its uber-masculine character, D'Argo, spent an entire episode with an alien he assumed was male only to uncomfortably discover that she was the female of her species and was considered quite beautiful on her homeworld. D'Argo awkwardly backed out of her flirtatious proposition.

We can discuss that old SNL gag, "It's Pat!" You might remember this; they even made a (pretty bad) movie about it. The running joke was that no one could tell if Pat was a man or a woman, which drove people around Pat crazy. They didn't know what to do with a person of unidentifiable gender, and their efforts to discover Pat's gender never produced a result. Comedy ensued.

What if Pat had announced themself to be gender-fluid or gender-neutral? That's the end of the sketch, I guess. But at the time, those answers were not a consideration.

I don't know if that SNL sketch displays a problematic old way of thinking or a brilliant depiction of the confusion experienced when we cannot place someone as a particular sex or assign them a gender role. We meet a new person, take in the dimensions of their body and facial features, and immediately check off the box. Male or female? And if we can't tell, we're so uncomfortable that it's fodder for a comedy sketch or a science fiction show. Has it ever happened to you? Have you ever accidentally called someone "sir" when it should have been "ma'am?" How embarrassing! How awful to mistake someone for the "wrong" sex and, by implication, the wrong gender.

We're trapped in sturdy ideas of our own culture's making.

WHAT *BRIDGING THE GAP* COVERED

In *Bridging the Gap*, I wrote about the things that interfere with gender equity, like implicit and explicit biases, micro-aggressions, and the double-edged problem of imposter syndrome. I recommended how our homes and workplaces can move toward gender equity. Briefly, let's review the highlights, giving us a starting point to discuss universal gender equity.

Implicit (Unconscious) Bias

Biases cause non-fact-based decision-making that favors one group over others.

Implicit biases are subconscious attitudes that alter our feelings and perceptions about other people. We absorb these beliefs almost from birth, from how our guardians speak to us, to our first social experiences, to our keen observations about the world around us.

Implicit bias is:

1. **Universal.** We all do it. Knowing that it happens puts you in a position to improve things.

2. **Hard to spot.** It's buried deep and often disguised as something else. Implicit biases are personal, and we may not like the presence of these unpleasant opinions in ourselves. We eagerly excuse our behaviors as the result of perfectly logical arguments.

3. **Systemic.** Implicit bias can be so long-standing and ordinary that we have codified the behaviors into

our lives and jobs, built into processes and programs. That is when "systemic" bias exists.

Types of Implicit Bias

This is by no means a definitive list, but here we have some biases that come into play when dealing with gender equity in the workplace.

Affinity Bias. We naturally gravitate toward people who are similar to us. We are more likely to hire or promote someone with the same traits.

Attribution Bias happens when we see a person as less competent due to gender. We undervalue what they have achieved and place undue emphasis on their mistakes.

Caregiver Bias. Not only do women shoulder the majority of childcare responsibilities, but they are also expected to care for elderly relatives.

Confirmation Bias. We favor information that supports what we already believe – meaning we notice, remember, and reference what supports our beliefs.

Halo/Horns Effect means we change how we perceive a person based on one characteristic, experience, or information. Thanks to the Confirmation Bias, we also notice and remember information that coincides with our biases.

Motherhood Bias. We believe that mothers are less reliable, less productive workers. Women who are mothers have lower salaries, get fewer promotions, and receive fewer job offers. Meanwhile, working *fathers* make 119% more than childless men (the "fatherhood bonus").

Prove-It-Again Bias. Women must provide far more evidence of competence than men; they must work twice as hard without guaranteeing they will be rewarded equally. Their work is scrutinized more critically and more often than that of men, and their mistakes count harder against them.

Tightrope Bias. We encourage and reward men for behaviors that we criticize from women. An admirable "take-charge" attitude in a man may be considered "bossy," "bitchy," or "uppity" for a woman. Unfortunately, we also penalize women for displaying behaviors associated with femininity. There lies the tightrope: Don't act like a man, and certainly don't act like a woman.

Woman's Work Bias. This is occupational segregation, referring to the fact that work done by women is generally undervalued. This bias accounts for half the disparity between gender earnings.

Microaggressions

Microaggression is the manifestation of bias in the workplace. These are subtle interactions, comments, or behaviors that express a bias toward a group that has been historically marginalized. They can be intentional or unintentional actions, and they can be verbal, behavioral, or environmental.

Microaggressions come in many guises, so let's review the various terms used to describe the most usual suspects:[1]

Microinsult. A microinsult often comes in the awkward form of a compliment. "You're pretty organized for a woman." "Most women bosses are so serious, but you're funny." "You work just as hard as the guys." The implication is that the target of the compliment is an exceptional case among her group.

Microinvalidation. A microinvalidation dismisses the experience of its victim, a member of a group with historical disadvantages, by implying that they are not disadvantaged at all, that their disadvantages aren't serious, or that, in any case, we don't care. We treat the victimized group as "invisible," refusing to acknowledge the problem.

Microassault. The microassault is deliberate mistreatment intended to marginalize or diminish the victim(s). This is bullying, belittling behavior, or any actions or language

---

1 https://www.baker.edu/about/get-to-know-us/blog/examples-of-workplace-microaggressions-and-how-to-reduce-them/

implying that the victim is inferior and unworthy, such as eye-rolling, nicknaming, interrupting, dismissing, or mocking.

Post-COVID remote work opportunities

In the post-pandemic work environment, flexibility in choosing "how we work" is more available than ever. Many workplaces now offer remote and flex positions in addition to office positions. Flexibility is vital to workplace diversification; our new work models provide more flexibility than workers have ever experienced.

But the new working reality of flextime has drawbacks. Without awareness and preparation for those drawbacks, the prevalence of flextime has the potential to put women (and other marginalized groups) in positions of diminishing power.

Women and other minorities are more likely to need and gravitate toward the advantages of flex-work and remote-work schedules. Disproportionately, women are responsible for child and elder care. Thus flextime and remote work are valuable to them. Marginalized employees, who may fear discrimination in the workplace, are also more likely to seek remote work.

The "pros" of remote work:

- Provides unheard-of opportunities for disabled persons.

- Opens up the scope and diversity of possible applicants for jobs.

The "cons" of remote work:

- We believe that people who come to the office are working harder. Flextime and remote workers are seen less and thus perceived as less hard-working.

- Facetime is a powerful way to foster relationships. Managers grow to know and like the people they see every day. Connections with flex and remote workers are not as strong.

- People working in the office have more opportunities, especially for mentorship, training, and education.

- Most essential employees and healthcare workers cannot do their jobs remotely.

Mental Health in the Workplace

Mental health is an essential part of a diverse and inclusive workplace. Inequity, exclusion, and microaggressions are highly stressful and burden employees' mental health. Where mental health goes, physical health follows, so employers should have a vested interest in keeping their workers' mental well-being in mind.

In my experience, there is a noticeable difference in employee happiness when DEI is thoroughly implemented in the system. I see amazing results when an employer offers a comprehensive suite of benefits, like medical, employee assistance programs (EAPs), and COPE Programs that promote both use and confidentiality.

- **Show employees that their well-being is essential.** Don't promise that "we're all a family here," but treat employees like machine tools. Employees intuit quickly how much a workplace truly cares for them.

- **Mental health coverage should be part of the healthcare plan.** The Mental Health Parity and Addiction Equity Act requires that insurance coverage for mental health conditions and substance abuse disorders is as accessible as, and no more limited than, coverage for other medical/surgical benefits.

- **Employers should use their power to ensure mental healthcare is a reality.** Employers are in the position to leverage their influence, building networks of equitable mental healthcare that are accessible and affordable to their employees.

- **Utilize managers as the "frontline" workers for mental health.** Managers are on the "frontline" and should be the ones who recognize and address mental healthcare needs in a time of crisis. Therefore, managers must be educated and empowered to identify and take action when they see someone struggling.

- **Develop an Employee Assistance Program (EAP) that supports mental health *confidentially and free of charge*.** Sending out a monthly newsletter that reminds employees of the benefits available to them, along with giving instructions on who to speak with and where to start, will help increase EAP usage and de-stigmatize the use of the confidential program.

- **Prepare for times of crisis by making emergency dollars available to your employees.** Sometimes, the best cure for stress is paying a pending bill or making a trip to the grocery store. Review your retirement plan activity to accommodate the need for loans during times of increased possibility for financial difficulties.

- **Provide opportunities for strong interpersonal connections in the workplace.** A job situation that feels like a "home away from home" can be a refuge because not all stressors happen at work.

<u>Imposter Syndrome</u>

Imposter syndrome (sometimes called "imposter phenomenon") can happen to anyone. It is typical for high achievers who forget the sheer amount of effort and time devoted to a cause because they look forward only to what is next, what is unfinished, and what they have not yet done. As you might expect, the phenomenon is prominently seen in underrepresented populations.

A certain amount of self-doubt is not only expected but healthy and a great motivator. A supportive work culture appreciates and nurtures self-doubt. But there is also an apparent difference between healthy self-doubt that saves us from making mistakes of overconfidence and the doubt that wheedles its way in because a hundred subconscious cues brand one as an outsider.

Though imposter syndrome is not limited to women or working, it has become a popular workplace diagnosis for working women in the past few decades. Women have plenty of good reasons to doubt their success, and those reasons have nothing to do with their internal landscapes. They are in work environments that need to change.

From a corporate perspective, there are ways to repair the broken systems that make our employees feel like they do not deserve success. The answer is to accept and promote that leadership comes in all shapes, sizes, colors, and genders. Leadership is not Eurocentric, masculine, and heteronormative; it is anyone who is a good leader. Strong leaders show the following traits:

1. Focus on developing/empowering others.

2. Excellent communication.

3. Strong team-building skills.

4. Knowing how to delegate.

5. Giving credit where it is due.

6. Behaving with integrity; being fair and ethical.

7. Enthusiasm and vision – the ability to inspire.

I see nothing on that list that is a masculine or feminine trait, nothing that requires 80 hours a week and no personal life, nothing that requires a certain age, skin color, or even education.

<u>Authenticity</u>

I am fortunate to work with various industries, companies of different sizes, and a remarkable variety of people daily. Seeing different perspectives and switching up my day that way is lovely. My favorite part of the job is learning from others.

I always impart to my clients the meaning of diversity, equity, and inclusion.

- Diversity encompasses everyone. All people differ from one another.

- Equity is the fair treatment, access, opportunity, and advancement for all people.

- Inclusion is creating a culture and environment that recognizes, appreciates, and effectively utilizes the talent, skills, and perspectives of everyone.

If there were one thing I would do to change people's minds, it would be this thought: **authenticity is critical**. Seeing the whole person is vital. So much more of us exists outside of the nine-to-five workday. Asking someone to stifle that part of themselves does not create a stellar employee.

I also remind my clients that intention and support *matter*. Rolling out a strategy or program to solve DEI problems falls flat when its intentions are insincere or unspecific and can only do good if supported throughout the organization.

Solutions for the Workplace

Gender equity begins with equitable hiring – hiring all genders for the same amount. But it also means that all genders are given the same opportunities once they are there.

Companies committed to diverse leadership have:

- A greater talent pool to access – more experience, more cultural fluency, more global thinking.

- Improved customer orientation and representation – consumers and partners gravitate toward businesses that react to their needs, lifestyles, backgrounds, etc. The consumer base grows more diverse with the company's diversity.

- Improved employee satisfaction – employees feel safer, stay longer, work better, and display loyalty to places where they feel valued and supported.

- Better decision-making processes – when hiring and promotion decisions are based on supportable facts, not feelings, this practice spreads throughout the culture.

Pay Transparency

I believe in wage transparency. Companies must implement transparent pay brackets.

One 2019 study from PayScale, a compensation data and software firm, found that among companies whose female employees described a transparent pay process, women were estimated to earn between $1 and $1.01 for every dollar earned by men.

Equity initiatives must be rewarded

Equity must be a core value at every level of an organization. To that point, companies must recognize and reward DEI efforts. Equity initiatives should be part of job descriptions and be acknowledged in performance reviews and formal evaluations. Results must be tied to incentives and material consequences, treated with as much value as the initiatives that increase sales or decrease absenteeism.

Standardized and formalized processes

Because unconscious bias is hard to spot and change in people, behavioral design means de-biasing organizations rather than individuals. Processes within organizations that require de-biasing include job descriptions, interviews, performance reviews, and promotion considerations. We must discover where breakdowns occur and find ways to eliminate or decrease the process's opportunities for bias.

The steps toward de-bias processes are:[2]

1. Use data and analytics to identify the processes that are bias-prone. The numbers will tell you when something is going on.

2. Standardize/formalize that process. You want to remove as much subjectivity as possible.

3. Expect that decision-making will require explanation and transparency. Hiring, promotions, and performance reviews must be supported with evidence that can be shown and explained to others.

Remember, taking the bias out of decision-making means making better decisions!

You can recruit with intention. Thanks to technology and

---

2 Tackling unconscious gender bias in the workplace – Ericsson.

the possibilities of remote workers, your applicant pool has dramatically expanded – take advantage of this. Reach out to the fantastic talent pool of diverse applicants. Then, let them know they are welcome in your culture and opportunities exist.

Adapt to the new normal:

- Allow workers to determine how they work best, then support their decision with the resources and information they need to be successful.

- Ensure that the same opportunities are available to remote, flex, and office workers.

- Engage employees in the work environment and community.

- Establish relationships with remote/flex workers, including regular contact.

- In addition to DEI training, form resource groups, sponsorship/mentorship programs, and workplace community-building efforts.

- Track and measure equity in hiring, promotions, and the performance review process, employee satisfaction, engagement, and the access and use of benefits and opportunities.

- Hold management, officers, and directors accountable for positive equity results. Senior-level sponsorship is vital.

MOVING OUR MINDSETS

Gender is currently a landmine issue. Humans are uncomfortable with changes in the status quo (which is a subjective thing already). Anytime a group of people decides to stop hiding its truth and announce, "Yes, we are different in this way, and yes, we're still humans, so we would like to be treated as such," there seems to be a backlash of staunch resistance.

Resistance flares, crying out, "No, you can't be human that way: something declares it wrong or impossible. You don't get the same rights as a human would, and you don't get the same treatment as humans would, and you certainly can't go around acting in your un-human way at the risk of infecting other good humans. Your un-humanness frightens, offends, and confuses me." Unfair though it may be, resistance is at least out in the open. We can see it. We know where the land-mines are. We can oppose it.

I work in DEI; my job and my calling is to promote equity. Explicit bias can be labeled and expressly forbidden in a workplace environment. Believe it or not, we're still working on that as issues, like pay inequity, continue to be a problem.

But the more stubborn enemy is implicit bias, which we all have and sneaks out so subtly that we may not recognize it for what it is. Explicit bias can be addressed with laws and regulations, but real change only occurs once implicit bias is found and compensated for.

This book is for those who know we must recognize our unconscious and systemic biases to create welcoming, safe environments for all genders, not just in the workplace but everywhere. In essence, we want to acknowledge that human gender is a landscape of differences and, in accepting it, stop making such a big deal out of it.

In *Bridging the Gap*, I wrote about normalizing women in leadership positions to the point that it's not a "wow" moment or something to remark upon when a woman manages a Fortune 500 company. Often there is an undercurrent of, "Oh, how amazing that a woman can handle this stressful leadership role!" or "How does she manage to balance her work life with her home life?" or an inordinate focus on her "soft" qualities – compassion, empathy, intuition. That kind of thinking is more systemic bias creeping in. We congratulate women for doing "men's work."

Normalization means taking gender out of the equation. That means all genders.

So, to start, let us remember that "gender" is not a synonym for "sex." Gender is how we identify ourselves and how others identify themselves.

The subject only gets complex and heated when we attempt to tell others that they don't know themselves well enough to know their gender, when we resist understanding, or when we believe that acknowledging "otherness" is somehow a detrimental thing.

In *Bridging the Gap*, I mainly focused on equity in the workplace. Now, in this book, I want to focus on equity in all aspects of our lives; social relationships, teams and groups, family life, community, and yes, the workplace too. So here we go. We're already making progress just by wanting to learn more.

Let's begin with the basics: by defining the terms used in 2023 to describe sex, gender, and sexual preferences.

♥

CHAPTER TWO:
THE IDENTITY INDEX

To begin a productive discussion on gender equity, we must know what we and others mean when referring to gender identities. So let's look at the various important terms used for biological sex, gender identities, and sexual orientation.

Note, many of these words are umbrella terms used to define generalizations. Any of these definitions can come with exceptions. Also, there are numerous sub-categories within some of these groups, and I will not include all of them here because these can get quite specific, and we would never make it to the next chapter of this book. For the definition of a term not listed below, you will find that the Human Rights Coalition website (hrc.org) has a great deal of information on the sub-groups of the LGBTQ+ community.

The meanings of the following words are current as of 2023, but the gender movement is fluid, and so are the words we use to discuss it. I am interested to see how definitions and new terms evolve in years to come. I have included some words that are no longer appropriate or accurate because we may still inadvertently use these terms without realizing they come with negative connotations or that they incorrectly categorize the people they attempt to describe.

I have also included the various flags used to represent communities because they are beautiful and tell surprising stories through their use of color. Encapsulated in stripes, their colors simplify community definitions and may help clarify a term's meaning. As you will see, the flags evolve alongside the gender movement.

Agender – one who has no gender, an unidentifiable gender, or is gender neutral. 
The evocative Agender flag was designed in 2014 by Salem X. Its black and white banners are meant to evoke gender absence, the gray represents a semi-genderlessness, and a green stripe represents the nonbinary.

Ally – a heterosexual or cisgender person who supports the LGBTQ+ civil rights movement and the equality of all gender identifications.

Asexual – A low, or absent, desire for sex and sexual activity. The reasons for low or absent desire may be phys- ical, emotional, intellectual, or any combination. An asexual person is 
usually not interested in anyone on a sexual level and typically does not experience sexual desires regardless of sexual ori- entation. These people are known as "Ace" or "Aces." Asexual does *not* mean one lacks gender identification or is intersex; it describes the absence of sexual orientation or disinterest in sexual activity.

Created in 2010, the asexual flag's black stripe indicates asexuality itself. It is followed by a literal "gray area" for gray- sexuality and demisexuality, a white stripe for asexual part- ners and asexual allies, then purple for the community.

Binary – In English, "binary" describes a system where two things exist exclusively, like the binary math system of ones and zeros. In the case of humans, we refer to the traditional gender binary, the classification of gender in two distinct forms: masculine and feminine. This is no longer considered correct, however. Though people have traditionally identified themselves (and others) as either masculine or feminine, as self-reflection on gender and sexuality continues, increasing numbers of people fall outside of this binary.

Bisexual – A bisexual person finds sexual or romantic attraction to both people of one's same sex and the opposite sex, or to people with the same or opposite gender identity as  oneself. "Bi" means "two," but it can also refer to "more than one." It is similar to, but not quite as broad a term as "pansexual," because while a bisexual may feel attraction to two or more sexes/genders, they do not necessarily feel attraction to all sexes and genders.

On the Bisexual flag (created in 1998), each band represents a possible attraction. Pink represents an attraction to the same sex. Blue represents an attraction to the opposite sex. Purple, of course, represents an attraction to both.

Chromosomes – These tiny little threads of nucleic acid and protein are found in living cells' nuclei. They carry our genetic information. Genetically, humans are made male or female by their chromosome pattern. On the DNA strand, males have the X and Y chromosomes, females have two X chromosomes, and there are also intersex variations of the chromosomal pattern. Chromosomes exist in every cell of a living creature's body.

Cisgender *(often abbreviated "Cis")* – By definition, this is the opposite of transgender. This term means that a person feels like their sex matches the sex they were assigned at birth: "The doctor got it right!" They are comfortable and identify with the sexual characteristics they were born with. However, one can still be cisgender and gay, for example, because this term refers only to one's gender, and not one's sexual orientation. Sometimes, LGBTQ+ communities use the term Cis to refer to people who follow common societal purviews.

Cross-Dresser. A cross-dresser is a person who wears clothing and adornments typical of the opposite sex. This is not synonymous with "drag" because cross-dressing does not always involve theatrical themes.

Demisexual refers to a person feeling sexual attraction only for those with whom a close emotional relationship exists – so they do not respond with attraction based on physical characteristics or their other early impressions of a person. Demisexuality encompasses any and all sexual orientations.

Drag. This term refers to a performer who adopts a glamorous costume, makeup and persona to imitate, parody or hyper-emphasize the traditional characteristics of a gender. An impressively large array of "drag" subcategories encompasses the wide variety of possibilities: Drag Queen and Drag King are only the beginning.

Gay – Sexual or romantic attraction to people of one's same sex. Gay can be anything related outside of the common "straight" sexuality, referring to anyone on the sexual spectrum. It has become a general term for anything that isn't straight and usual, along with the LGBTQ+ community as a whole.

Gay Pride – Or simply "Pride," this term promotes self-affirmation, dignity, equality, and increased visibility of the LGBTQ+ community as a social group. It's reasonable to see Gay Pride as a civil rights movement.

The Gay Pride or Rainbow Pride flag generally represents the LGBTQ+ community as a whole. The design was created by Gilbert Baker in 1978 at the request of activist Harvey Milk.

Currently, the flag most often used is this six-striped version: red represents life, orange represents healing, yellow represents sunlight, green represents nature, blue represents harmony and serenity, and purple represents the community.

The original Gilbert Baker Pride flag included a hot pink stripe (representing sexuality) and two shades of blue: turquoise (for art) and indigo (for serenity).

Gender – Traditionally, this was how one's culture defines sexual orientation and applies masculine and feminine traits to girls and boys. However, modern gender definitions have changed. Gender now describes how a person identifies themselves regardless of their birth-assigned sex. Gender is a broad spectrum, and people may define themselves within or outside it.

Gender Fluid – A person who describes themselves as "gender fluid" would rather identify and express themselves through their gender orientation than their sexual orientation  and sexual characteristics, but more importantly, that gender is not necessarily consistent. Gender-fluid people may adopt different genders over time; they do not exclusively identify as male, female, or other.

The Gender Fluid flag was created by JJ Poole in 2012. Its stripes represent the various stages of gender fluidity: pink for feminine and blue for masculine, with purple for both masculine and feminine, white for all genders, and black for no gender or lack of gender.

Gender Identity – One's innermost concept of male, female, neither, both, or other – and there are many "others!" Gender identity is how a person perceives themselves and what they call themselves. This can be the same, or different, from their birth sex, and can encompass two or more genders (see Gender Fluid).

Gender Reassignment is the process (which usually involves a combination of surgical and hormonal treatments) of altering physical sexual characteristics to match gender identity. We used to call this procedure a "sex change operation," but we have adopted better terminology: now the surgical procedures involved may also be called "Gender Affirming Surgery," "Gender Confirmation Surgery," or "Sex Reassignment Surgery."

Genderqueer – is another term for a person whose gender identity does not correspond to a traditional binary gender distinction. One who identifies as genderqueer may identify as  both male and female, neither male nor female, or in a category outside of male/female. Genderqueer is a subcategory of non-binary persons.

The Genderqueer flag (2011, by Marilyn Roxie) represents androgyny, queer identities, agender, gender-neutral identities, and all that fall outside of the gender binary.

Graysexual is the term for people who are asexual but will still engage in sexual activity sporadically or occasionally.

Heterosexual – a straight person who is sexually or romantically attracted to people of the opposite sex. The prefix "hetero" is from the Greek *heteros*, which means, "the other (of two), another, different, second; other than usual."

Homosexual. The term "homosexual" was once defined in the same way as "gay," and was used interchangeably with "gay" to refer to a sexual orientation for same-sex partners. However, it is no longer used because it is problematic. The root word "homo" is derived from the Latin *hominis,* which means "human being" or "man." The word is not only incorrect but also has largely negative connotations.

Intersex. Intersex individuals are born with more than one of the biological male and female sexual characteristics. These may include having both male and female chromosomes, genitalia, or gonads. 

About one in every 2000 people born have intersex characteristics; it is a natural occurrence and not considered a medical problem. These characteristics may be apparent at birth, but may also not display until puberty, if at all. Intersex people may identify as either, both, or outside of, the binary masculine or feminine genders.

For many decades, when an intersex child was born with obvious physical differences, parents were pressured into "choosing" a sex and raising the child under those societal conceptions, which may have included surgical measures to remove or alter genitalia. This measure often led to serious physical and psychological scarring. Now the Human Rights Commission considers such surgery a human rights violation when it is done for cosmetic purposes only and without the individual's consent. Surgeries are only performed on intersex infants when there is physical danger, such as when the infant cannot urinate effectively. Parents of intersex children now allow their children to choose if and when surgical alterations may be performed when they are old enough to make informed consent.

The Intersex flag is noticeably different from other LGBTQ+ community flags. Yellow and purple are used because they have no gender connotations, and the perfect circle implies wholeness and completeness. It was designed in 2013 by Morgan Carpenter.

Lesbian – Denotes and relates to women who are sexually or romantically attracted to other women. Lesbians also use the term "gay" to indicate being outside the norm.  The Lesbian flag has many permutations. This particular example is a more modern addition to the flag iconography. Tumblr blogger Emily Gwen designed it in 2018. Each band's color is special in the lesbian community, such as womanhood, independence, non-conformity, and femininity.

LGBT – This is a simplified abbreviation. Its letters are from defined gay terms Lesbian, Gay, Bisexual, and Transgender. LBGT is often used to reference gay communities, media, and organizations.

LGBTQ – As the gay community is ever-evolving, so is their abbreviation. This abbreviation adds the Q from Queer to LGBT and is now used about as commonly as the acronym LGBT.

LGBTQ+ – People continually define and discover how they feel, and how they identify themselves.

At one point, the evolving LGBT abbreviation became a little too long as more terms were identified and added to the community, to where the abbreviation was listed as LGBTQIA, which added Questioning or Queer, Intersex, and Asexual. Then, more and more terms were proposed to be added to the abbreviation, each term originating from different communities and adding to the abbreviation.

This would eventually defeat the purpose of an abbreviation, so a plus was added onto the end of LGBT or LGBTQ in order to signify any identities and orientations that people would like to associate with the gay community.

Non-Binary refers to anyone who identifies outside the binary system of male/female. When someone calls themself "non-binary," they do not wish to identify themselves in the tra-  ditional purview of male or female. They can define themselves and express themselves accordingly without following typical masculine or feminine iconography. It includes gender-queer, intersex, and bisexuality.

Created in 2014 by Kye Rowan, the Non-Binary flag's wide spectrum of colors represents the wide possibility of gender identification. Yellow represents gender outside the binary, white represents people with many/all genders, purple represents a mix of male/female genders, and black represents people who identify as having no gender.

Pansexual – This term refers to one who feels a sexual or romantic attrac-tion to others regardless of the others' sex or gender identity. Pansexuality does not have a preference for either  gender or sexual characteristics when determining attraction toward others.

The Pansexual flag, created in the early 2010s by Jasper V, represents attraction to males (blue) and females (pink), with the importance of a yellow nonbinary attraction in the middle.

Progress Pride is the movement to increase inclusiveness in the LGBTQ+ community to acknowledge margin-alized groups such as gay people of color and transgender people. 

The Progress Pride flag is a lovely representation of this inclusion. The original Pride flag now includes the oncoming arrow of colors. Light blue, light pink, and white represent transgender and non-binary people. The brown and black stripes stand for marginalized communities of color. The black stripe is also considered a tribute to those who live with or have died from AIDS.

This flag's even more up-to-date version, developed in 2021, now includes the Intersex community's symbol.

Queer – Like the term "non-binary," queer refers to those people who see themselves as falling outside of the norm both in sexuality and gender norms.

Questioning – This person feels as if they don't follow sexual and gender norms, yet is unsure how to define their feelings or which term may best describe them.

Sex – Refers to the physiological differences between humans who are male, female, or intersex. This is typically assigned at birth based on characteristics centered around genitalia and chromosome composition. Assigned sex is sometimes called "natal sex." A person's biological sex is immutable – it is determined on a genetic level during fertilization and embryonic development. Perhaps we should add here that biological sex is immutable *presently* – and for the foreseeable future – but I won't assume that this will *never* be possible, for example, through advances in gene therapy.

Sexual Reassignment – is another fairly common term for gender reassignment.

Straight – The traditional description of someone having a sexual orientation to persons of the opposite sex, as in heterosexual.

Transexual – Relating or denoting a transgender person, especially if they have undergone gender reassignment.

Transgender or Trans – A person who does not follow the gender identity of the sex assigned to them at birth. One does not need to receive a sex change in order to be called "trans." 
The Trans flag's blue and pink lines represent the traditional colors associated with baby girls and boys. Therefore, the white line in the center represents a transition or bridge between the two identities – and because it is symmetrical, it is a clever representation of being correct, no matter which side is up! This flag was first designed by Monica Helms in 1999.

Transvestite. Traditionally, this term referred to a cross-dresser, but it is no longer considered appropriate because of derogatory connotations.

CONCLUSION

Languages are fluid and constantly evolving. Every year new words appear, and old words fade into obscurity, relating to all aspects of our lives. New terms for gender and sexuality may initially seem confusing or even pointless – particularly if we have trouble understanding the underlying emotions, thoughts, or physiology involved. In later chapters, we will look more closely at how we can support equity for any and all genders, including accepting the terms with which communities define themselves.

♥

CHAPTER THREE:
LEARNING AND UNLEARNING
GENDER ROLES

The question of "when" we first learn about gender is difficult to pinpoint because no two of us are raised from infancy in the same way. Generally, children begin understanding physical gender differences after the age of two. By the time they are three, they show behaviors that conform to the expected behaviors of a gender. They may choose games or toys that we perceive as "masculine" or "feminine." (Now take care – because those terms are already socially decided constructs – that dolls are feminine, that trucks are masculine.)

A child's choices in clothing may veer toward what seems gender-appropriate. They may show preferences for playing with same-sex friends. Then, by the age of five or six, a child has a fixed idea of gender, but this is based on what their society tells them is correct – in effect, it is when children become thoroughly socialized.

It is nearly impossible to separate nature from nurture when it comes to deciphering whether or why a child acts like what we think of as a boy, a girl, or neither. So many factors come into play when establishing gender roles. We can look at society, the language we use, the people who have contact with the child (not just parents but grandparents and other relatives, friends, teachers, and acquaintances), and the media children are exposed to.

The cues that children receive about their behavior and preferences can be blatantly obvious or incredibly subtle, to the point where such things happen on an almost subconscious level. It does not require outright praise. "Congratulations on acting like a boy!" It can be a nod, a microexpression, or the mere lack of disapproval, which says to a child, "You are acting in the way I'd expect you to act. Carry on."

We have generations of social training that assumed "boys will be boys and girls will be girls" without ever realizing that some children might feel like both or neither or that it is unfair to expect a child to conform to the gender roles that are in large part arbitrarily decided by culture. And as I discussed in Chapter One, we have only relatively recently realized that "sex" and "gender" are not the same thing. Sex may be biological, but gender is conceptual.

So first, the difficulty. If a child is raised within a society, avoiding all societal expectations of gender stereotypes cannot happen. A society's norms will convey to that child what is expected of their gender, including behavior, appearance, and preferences. The desire to conform is a reasonably strong one; most of us want to fit in.

Therefore, our society's movement away from gender stereotypes is a positive one. We began a few decades ago by breaking masculine and feminine stereotypes down. We no longer think in terms of "men's jobs" or "women's jobs" but simply jobs. There aren't "father roles" and "mother roles" but "parental roles." Note, however, that I said "began" because as much progress as we have made, we still have a long way to go when it comes to gender equity in the workplace. And once more, we face this problem: many of us still think of "gender equity" in terms of exclusively two genders. We continue to subject women to a variety of gender biases in the workplace and continue to undervalue their work and contributions. The more marginalized the person is (if they identify as a woman and are also Black, and also gay or trans), the more bias they suffer. We need to take a page from common parental recommendations and move them into our adult lives.

But let's not discount that progress has been made. We can observe progress in the way parents are guided to interact with their genderqueer, gender-neutral, or questioning children.

THE BASICS, BEGINNING WITH CHILDHOOD

Our purpose here is not to create a guide to raising children, but I will mention the current slate of recommendations given to parents on the subject of raising their children to understand gender neutrality. I do so for a number of reasons:

- Because these recommendations demonstrate an age level at which gender roles are generated and what kinds of behaviors promote specific gender roles.

- However, they *also* show an interesting paradox: letting a child be themselves is relatively easy while avoiding all gender role expectations from society is practically impossible – or at least it is at present.

- The most important thing we can do is show ourselves as allies. We support and defend the choices children make about their gender.

- And these recommendations work equally well for adults. If you are making an honest effort to restructure your thinking about gender, take these to heart. There's nothing about the following recommendations that applies to parents and children alone.

Help kids understand that any gender can excel in any topic. We eliminate anything like "boys are better at math and sports" or "girls are better at reading and cooking" preconceptions. Regardless of their gender, no child should be discouraged from pursuing an interest just because it doesn't fit traditional ideas of what is appropriate. Allow children to choose their passions.

Help kids break gender stereotypes by encouraging them to be friends with everyone and encouraging play with a variety of objects – let all children have access to anything they like without imposing masculine or feminine characteristics onto the child or the toys.

Praise all children for the same behaviors; likewise, discourage undesirable behavior equally. If you'd expect a little girl to be still while a little boy is allowed to squirm and tumble because "that's how boys are," this is sending a gender message. Expect everyone to sit still or let everyone squirm and tumble without bringing gender into it. It's as simple as that. If being assertive or opinionated is a desirable quality for a boy, then it is for a girl as well. If kindness and generosity are encouraged in young women, encourage them equally in young men.

Use gender-neutral terms like "police officer," "firefighter," and "chairperson." That part is pretty straightforward. But be careful about pronouns too – we sometimes tell stories or explain situations about authority figures, always using the pronouns "he/him," as if we assume automatically that a doctor, judge, or CEO will be a man. Try to remember to use "they/them" for a hypothetical person.

Encourage books, games, and other media that are gender-neutral or show people taking on nontraditional roles.

Answer questions as they arise, and don't make a big deal out of little things. You will not destroy a child's gender perceptions by accidentally assuming a nuclear physicist must be a man. In fact, when you make a mistake, say so out loud. "I assumed the scientist would be a man, but there was no reason to think that, was there?"

Parents are also given direction on communicating with

children who may be gender diverse. **Gender incongruence** is a term used when one's gender feels like it doesn't match one's biological sex. Some children express diversity from quite a young age; others may begin to feel gender diversity when they are older. It is not unusual for a child to "experiment" with opposite-gender behaviors, but this does not necessarily mean gender diversity.

A major concern for parents of gender-diverse children is isolation, prejudice, and bullying against their child – because acceptance of gender diversity is still in its relative infancy. As much as we parents would like to shelter our children from all harm, most of the time, we must expose them to a world where not everything is fair or just.

When a child is gender-diverse, parents are encouraged:

- To communicate without judgment.

- Not to shame the gender expression.

- Not to allow others to shame or ridicule the child's gender expression.

- To allow the child to express gender in public.

- To use language that affirms the gender (this includes respecting a child's preferred name and pronouns).

- To express positivity and pride in a child's expression of their identity.

So, once more, let's look at what parents do for a gender-diverse child. This is behavior that applies to adult social situations. We may be dealing with a friend or coworker rather than our own child, but the standards of conduct change little, if at all.

THE BASICS, CONTINUING WITH LANGUAGE

Allowing someone to express their gender(s) or lack of gender is not difficult. The thing is, if we stop and consider most of the people we know and interact with on a daily basis, we may quickly find that their gender is irrelevant to whether a job is done correctly, expediently, brilliantly, and so on. We have gender ingrained into our perceptions of others only because we were taught to perceive people that way.

In the past few decades, online communication has presented an interesting new spin on relationships: the ability to become associated with, friendly with, or even dependent on, other human beings without ever seeing or hearing them. Entire communities may form online without anyone having a definite idea of the gender (age, race, or anything else) of the people with whom they associate. United in a cause, they find that such details are irrelevant. And while it is true that the anonymity of online relationships can lead to scamming, dishonesty is not the exclusive territory of anonymity.

If I wanted someone to type a 30-page document for me, I could go to Upwork or Fiverr and hire a worker based entirely on their resume, get the work done, and pay them without necessarily ever knowing their gender. Granted, names are often gender-indicative, but not always, and as usual, it is unwise to make assumptions. Do I care whether my work was done by a man, a woman, or someone who identifies as both or neither? It makes no difference if the job is done correctly. In fact, it makes no difference even if the job is done incorrectly. Gender is not a relevant factor.

When gender seems to get relevant is when we're facing it head-on. That's a personal bias, but there it is. We have learned to see the human race as divided into two groups: male/masculine and female/feminine, though we have grown our perception to include gay people because we have learned to accept different sexual preferences. But now gender has risen as a new issue, and not so many years ago, most of us didn't even know it could actually be one. "What's the issue?" we might have asked. "How can there be an issue? You're a man or a woman, right?" We admit that we know someone who knew someone who had a sex change operation, not that there's anything wrong with that.

Okay, let's begin with *unlearning* gender roles. You grew up believing there were two genders. That was wrong. It's okay that it was wrong. There are many things we believe to be right that are later proven false. We thought for a long time that poor Pluto was a planet. It's not. We believed that nothing could escape a black hole. It can. You don't have to do this overnight; you don't have to get it perfect right off the bat. But there's no fair reason to uphold old beliefs simply because that's what you grew up with. We can open our minds to the notion that gender is more than we thought – and you'll find, amazingly, that once you get your head around gender, it gets simple again.

We'll look at this from the perspective of the workplace, but like the advice about allowing children to express their gender freely, applying not just to home and school, we must accept that this applies in all settings: home, work, social and group settings.

Here is a list of qualities I dearly love about my best friend.

1. I can talk to them about anything – they never judge my thoughts or feelings.

2. They always make me laugh, and vice versa. We're always cracking up.

3. They always make me look on the bright side.

4. They and I enjoy the same movies and tv shows, and we share some really in-depth, nerdy debates about these things that are always a blast.

5. Any activity we do – even routine things – is more fun because we are together.

6. I would be glad to defend their choices and preferences.

Now as I look over this list, I don't see anything that I can attribute to gender. Can you tell the gender of my best friend from the information I have given? In an upcoming chapter, we'll discuss how to support a friend or loved one who is in or considering joining the Gay Community.

Now let's look at how I feel about a valuable business relationship I have with a client.

1. They provide excellent, timely feedback.

2. They pay their invoices immediately.

3. They have brought several great projects to my attention.

4. They are specific about project goals so we can make quick progress.

What gender is my business associate? Does it matter?

For now, I want to emphasize that the majority of our valuable relationships are not genuinely gender-dependent. Where gender does play a role is when we talk about intimate relationships – and yes, at that point, your preferences are as valid as anyone else's. But if you're basing your opinions of coworkers, for example, not on their merits but on whether or not you find them physically attractive, you are already on a slippery slope of bias regardless of the genders involved. If this is a situation you face: "I cannot work with genderfluid people because I don't know whether or not I can or want to sleep with them," then you might need to reexamine your priorities about all relationships.

Language evolution: gender pronouns and beyond

They/them/themself.
He/him/himself.
She/her/herself.
Xe/xem/xemself.
Ze/zir/zirself.
Ze/hir/hirself.

There are many others – English currently has an incredible diversity of non-binary pronouns. In the future, we may settle on one or more sets to represent chosen gender or lack thereof.

Not so many years ago, we might never have imagined asking this question of anyone. "What's your name, and what are your pronouns?" We met a person, assumed a man/woman gender based on their appearance, and assumed he/him or she/her pronouns. Of course, we knew of prominent celebrity situations, like famous drag queens, in which the pronoun situation became more complex, and we understood that people who had sexual reassignment surgery would have pronoun changes, but in our ground-level, day-to-day interactions, there were two genders and we could pretty much bank on our assumption being the correct one.

Making this assumption now is impractical and unwise – denying someone their pronouns is denying their identity.

There is controversy, and even mockery, surrounding the issue of pronouns. Like any social change, it is met with resistance. If your personal beliefs tell you that letting people choose their pronouns is ridiculous, you may, in fact, be reading the wrong book. I'm speaking to people who are ready to accept that calling someone by the correct pronouns is respectful.

But I admit, there are those of us who are over a certain age who might find the new pronoun usage challenging, and we'll make mistakes at first. We learned our language in a particular way, and we learned how to use pronouns in a specific way. Non-binary pronouns are, indeed, a new twist on language for us. Here's how to cope:

- Remember, it's pretty easy. Pronoun usage is a pattern of speech, but language is extraordinarily flexible, and you'll be fine. A bit of practice and your marvelously elastic brain will get it.

- And when you do make a mistake, don't make a big deal out of it. It's rather like getting someone's name wrong. It's not precisely suave, but it's not the end of the world. Correct your mistake, apologize sincerely (but without throwing yourself on a pyre), and move on. Do better next time.

- Introducing yourself with your own pronouns will let others know it's okay to share theirs. Non-binary people may be hesitant to share their pronouns because they do not know what environment they are in, and the prejudice they face is often disheartening. If I introduce myself this way, "Hello, I'm Alexandra, and I use she/her," this says, "I care about your pronouns, too."

- You will note that many email signatures now come with pronoun preferences too. Consider including yours, which conveys the same message of inclusion as introducing yourself and including your pronouns.

- If you don't know someone's pronouns yet, "they/them" is the commonly accepted set of pronouns to use until you do. In addressing letters/emails, if you do not know someone's chosen gender, it is appropriate to use a simple "M." instead of "Mr., Mrs., Ms., or Miss." Mx. (pronounced Mix) may be the title to use for people who have chosen they/them as pronouns.

- When addressing a crowd, use gender-neutral terms like people, folks, attendees, friends, or devotees. "Ladies and gentlemen" doesn't do the trick any longer!

- "Ma'am" and "Sir" are no longer reliable to use for people whose gender you do not know. Now, this may be even harder for some of us than the change of pronouns because we were raised saying "Yes sir!" and "Yes ma'am!" like we were little soldiers in basic training. For decades these have been the appropriate responses in customer service, education, or just generally speaking to older people or people we respect. The best way to cope is to say something else that is not gender specific, "Yes, of course!" "Yes, my pleasure." "No, I'm sorry." If someone wants to be addressed as "sir" or "ma'am," they can certainly say so.

- English is not the only language where this evolution is happening; languages around the world recognize third-gender and non-binary pronouns. Portuguese and Spanish, French and German, Catalan and Chinese all have gender-neutral pronouns. Modern languages worldwide are adapting to include gender-neutral language.

- If all else fails, look up the answer. When in doubt, a quick internet search will give you the information you need. This may not guarantee that you're right 100% of the time, but earnest efforts are essential and meaningful.

CONCLUSION

Now, let's follow up on the purpose of this chapter, which was the learning and unlearning of gender. While our language does follow our thinking, you will be surprised how our thinking also follows our language. When we learn how to speak in terms of gender neutrality and we respect the terms people wish to use to refer to themselves, we have automatically paved the road for acceptance. We have begun to "unlearn" gender stereotypes.

♥

CHAPTER FOUR:
MEDIA IN THE DEI REVOLUTION

In today's evolving understanding and normalization of non-binary and transgender people, the media plays a pivotal role in shaping our perceptions and attitudes of the gay community. For individuals who identify as non-binary and transgender, media representation is not only crucial for validation but also for challenging societal norms and promoting inclusivity. In this chapter, we'll get a little starstruck while we look at the importance of outspoken celebrities and the media in bringing inclusivity to our society.

THE POWER OF REPRESENTATION

For those not part of the LGBTQ+ community, it may be difficult to understand why representation is such a crucial issue. However, imagine going through life constantly bombarded with images and narratives that do not reflect who you are. Consider the experience of attending a family gathering with your same-sex partner and being asked about marriage when marriage equality is not yet a reality. This constant erasure and invisibility can incredibly damage one's sense of self.

Representation matters because it validates and affirms the experiences of LGBT+ individuals. It shows them that they are not alone and that their stories are valid and worthy of being told. Seeing oneself represented on-screen goes beyond mere entertainment value; it is a robust validation of one's identity.

While media has progressed concerning representation, the media industry is still noticeably lopsided in specific capacities (news anchors, leading characters, "everyone is straight" sitcoms). Historically, mainstream media has tended to portray predominantly white, cisgender gay men and women, leaving out the experiences of other marginalized groups within the LGBTQ+ community. This lack of diversity perpetuates the idea that only certain identities are valid or worthy of representation. We mustn't forget that this is a two-way street. While it is true that we learn from the media, the media also responds to what we express interest in.

Thankfully, the rise of streaming platforms like Netflix, Stan, and SBS on Demand has provided opportunities for more diverse storytelling. Web series like *Brown Girls* and shows like *Transparent* and *The 100* have brought the experiences of queer people of color, transgender individuals, and bisexual characters to the forefront. These narratives challenge traditional norms and provide a more accurate reflection of the diversity within the LGBT+ community.

Authentic representation has a profound impact on both LGBTQ+ and non-LGBTQ+ audiences. For LGBTQ+ individuals, seeing themselves represented authentically on-screen can be empowering. It helps them understand that their experiences are valid and that they are not alone. It can also be a source of education for queer and straight individuals, fostering greater understanding and empathy.

Conversely, inaccurate or harmful representations can perpetuate stereotypes and further marginalize the LGBTQ+ community. For example, the "bury your gays" trope – more on this later – where writers frequently kill off queer characters can send a damaging message that queer lives are less valuable and queer characters less "missed" by those left behind. These harmful depictions can contribute to the mental health issues faced by the LGBTQ+ community, which sadly include higher rates of self-harm and suicide.

Media, including film and television, plays a significant role in shaping societal norms and beliefs. By portraying diverse and authentic LGBT+ characters and storylines, the media has the power to challenge stereotypes, break down barriers, and promote acceptance. It can help educate audiences about the wide range of experiences within the LGBTQ+ community and create a more inclusive and empathetic society.

The relationship between audiences and on-screen representations is impactful and informative. Whether it is direct representation or the interpretation of certain characters as queer, the on-screen images we consume can bring solace and acceptance or perpetuate isolation and ignorance. Achieving equality requires changing all avenues of representation, from the choices made by producers and writers to the images projected on our screens.

THE PEOPLE WE WATCH

In a world that has long been confined to the binary concept of gender, the rise of nonbinary celebrities has been nothing short of groundbreaking. These individuals, who do not identify exclusively as male or female, challenge societal norms and push the boundaries of gender identity. Their influence and visibility reshape the entertainment industry and foster a more inclusive and accepting society.

Nonbinary celebrities use their platforms and visibility to challenge societal norms and promote acceptance and understanding. Their presence in the media is breaking down barriers and providing much-needed representation for nonbinary individuals everywhere.

Let's take a look at some of these influential figures.

Janelle Monae is known for their mesmerizing performances and soulful music. They came out as nonbinary during an appearance on *Red Table Talk*. They use the pronouns they/

them and she/her and have expressed their commitment to standing with women, particularly Black women, on important issues. By sharing their nonbinary identity, Monae encourages others to embrace their authentic selves and challenges societal expectations.

Sam Smith, the Grammy-winning artist, made headlines when they came out as nonbinary in 2019. In an Instagram post, Smith expressed their journey of self-acceptance, stating that they no longer identify strictly as male or female but somewhere in between. By openly discussing their gender identity, Smith is promoting a more inclusive understanding of gender and inspiring others to embrace their true selves.

Emma D'Arcy, known for their role as Rhaenyra Targaryen in HBO's *House of the Dragon*, identifies as nonbinary. D'Arcy uses the pronouns they/them and has spoken about their experience of being pulled and repelled by masculine and feminine identities. By openly discussing their gender identity, D'Arcy is challenging societal norms and highlighting the complexity of gender.

Sara Ramirez, best known for their role as Callie Torres on *Grey's Anatomy*, came out as nonbinary on Instagram. Ramirez expressed their capacity to embody various gender expressions, stating they can be a "girlish boy, boyish girl, boyish boy, girlish girl, all, neither." Through their openness, Ramirez is advocating for a more fluid understanding of gender and encouraging others to embrace their authentic selves.

Jonathan Van Ness, the hair and grooming expert on *Queer Eye*, publicly identifies as nonbinary. In their interview with *Out* magazine, Van Ness discussed their gender nonconformity, stating that they feel more aligned with the nonbinary and gender nonconforming spectrum. By sharing their personal journey, Van Ness is promoting a more inclusive understanding of gender and advocating for self-acceptance.

Nico Tortorella, known for their role in *Younger*, came out as nonbinary in 2018. They openly discussed their self-discovery journey of realizing they are not fully cisgender. Tortorella's openness about their gender identity challenges societal norms and encourages others to explore and embrace their uniqueness.

Kehlani, an R&B singer, publicly identifies as nonbinary and uses the pronouns she/they. In an interview with Byrdie, Kehlani expressed their comfort when referred to as "they," as it feels affirming to them. By openly discussing their pronoun preferences, Kehlani raises awareness and promotes inclusivity in the music industry and beyond.

Lachlan Watson, known for their role as Susie Putnam in *Chilling Adventures of Sabrina*, initially came out as trans before realizing they were nonbinary. Watson's journey of self-discovery led them to the realization that their discomfort was not solely about being assigned female, but rather about the limitations imposed by societal norms. By sharing their story, Watson is challenging societal constructs and promoting self-acceptance.

Ruby Rose, known for their role in *Orange Is the New Black*, has spoken openly about their journey with gender. While not publicly identifying as nonbinary, Rose has discussed their androgynous identity and their fluidity with their gender. By embracing their androgyny, Rose challenges traditional gender norms and encourages others to embrace their unique identities.

Amandla Stenberg, an actor who is known for roles in *The Hunger Games* and *The Hate U Give,* goes by the pronouns she/they. Stenberg publicly shared their pronoun preferences on Tumblr, expressing that being referred to as "they" makes them feel comfortable. By openly discussing their pronouns, Stenberg promotes inclusivity and provides visibility for nonbinary individuals.

Dua Saleh, who is known for their role in *Sex Education*, identifies as nonbinary and uses the pronouns she/they. Saleh also introduced neopronouns, specifically xe/xyr/xim, to their social media presence. By embracing neopronouns, Saleh is challenging traditional gender language and advocating for a more inclusive understanding of identity.

Bella Ramsey gained recognition for her role as Lyanna Mormont in *Game of Thrones*. She recently revealed that she identifies as nonbinary. Ramsey shared that she uses any pronouns and expressed her enjoyment in playing female characters while emphasizing her dedication to her craft. By openly discussing her nonbinary identity, Ramsey challenges societal expectations and promotes individuality in the entertainment industry.

Nonbinary celebrities are playing a vital role in reshaping societal perceptions of gender. Their openness and visibility challenge traditional norms and foster a more inclusive and accepting society. Their influence extends beyond the entertainment industry, inspiring individuals to embrace their authentic selves and promoting empathy and respect for the diverse experiences of nonbinary individuals.

As we celebrate these nonbinary celebrities, we must recognize that gender is a deeply personal and individual experience. By embracing and supporting nonbinary identities, we can create a world where everyone feels seen, accepted, and celebrated for who they truly are.

THE STORIES WE LOVE

For most of us, the media plays a significant role. The truth is, characters we love become almost as real to us as the people we know, so examples of transgender and nonbinary fictional characters serve as a vital bridge. When the things that entertain us – books, theater, television, movies – show a diverse and inclusive world or draw our attention to biases and human rights issues, several things happen, including:

- We find common ground from which to approach these issues with others.

- We learn that transgender or non-binary people are simply people – normalizing rather than stigmatizing a group.

- We see that being a man or a woman specifically is not necessary to be a person worth knowing or caring about.

- We break down stereotypes, learning more nuanced portrayals of all genders.

Media non-binary and transgender representations challenge the traditional gender binary, expand our understanding of gender diversity, and validate the experiences and identities of non-binary individuals. They provide a sense of affirmation and belonging while reducing feelings of isolation. Representation also helps others understand and relate to non-binary individuals, fostering empathy and support and creating allies. Positive representation breaks down stereotypes and myths.

Thankfully, there has been progress in the representation of LGBTQ+ individuals in the media. In the 1990s, shows like *Will and Grace* and *Ally McBeal* featured groundbreaking portrayals of gay characters and even depicted same-sex kisses. These shows paved the way for more inclusive storytelling in the following decade.

In recent years, there has been a notable increase in non-binary representation on television and web series. It is no longer enough to have token gay characters or storylines that try to be representative but eventually only perpetuate stereotypes. The demand for authentic and diverse representation has grown, and for good reason. The way LGBTQ+ individuals are portrayed on-screen has a significant impact on their personal identities and overall well-being.

Shows like *Billions, Supergirl,* and *Brooklyn Nine-Nine* introduced non-binary characters, providing visibility and exploring their experiences. Web series such as *The Feels* and *Non-Binary Diaries* also emerged, focusing on non-binary stories and perspectives.

The film industry also makes positive strides in non-binary representation. Movies like *The Matrix Resurrections* and *The Craft: Legacy* feature non-binary characters, with actors who identify as non-binary portraying these roles.

Non-binary representation in literature has also gained traction. Award-winning authors like Akwaeke Emezi, Kacen Callender, and Alice Oseman craft stories for all age groups that feature non-binary characters, providing readers with relatable narratives and fostering understanding and acceptance.

The gaming industry is another primary source for normalization and inclusion. For decades, companies like *Bioware* have allowed characters to form romantic relationships with same-sex partners and make friends (and lovers) of individuals from non-binary worlds. Now, gaming has also embraced non-binary representation. Games like *The Last of Us Part II* and *Tell Me Why* feature non-binary characters as protagonists, allowing players to engage with their stories and experiences. Games that allow players to choose their avatar's sex now often include a non-binary option in addition to male/female, such as in 2023's release of *Baldur's Gate*.

Non-binary representation has also found a home on social media and online platforms. Content creators and influencers use their platforms to share their non-binary experiences, educate others, and advocate for inclusivity.

Non-binary representation should also strive for intersectionality and inclusivity. It is essential to feature non-binary characters from diverse racial, ethnic, and cultural backgrounds and non-binary individuals with disabilities and varying socioeconomic backgrounds. By doing so, the media can provide a more accurate reflection of the non-binary community's diversity and experiences.

Authenticity is paramount in non-binary representation,

which means that non-binary characters should be portrayed by non-binary actors whenever possible, or transgender characters by transgender actors, and so on. Representative casting ensures that these individuals' lived experiences and perspectives receive accurate representation, providing an authentic voice to the community.

WHEN DOES IT GO WRONG?

Despite the progress made, non-binary representation still faces challenges. Stereotypes and misconceptions can perpetuate harmful narratives, leading to misunderstandings and discrimination. Media must move away from these harmful portrayals and focus on authentic, diverse, and nuanced representations. We've come a long way from the profoundly offensive portrayals of nontraditional persons as crazy serial killers at worst and jokes at best. Despite tremendous progress, some deep-seated entertainment tropes still plague LGBTQ+ characters. You'll recognize these, and they are certainly not the only ones!

- **The gay best friend.** This trope is both progressive, as it includes gay characters in the story, and dismissive because it usually leaves an interesting gay man serving as only an accessory or an advisor to a heterosexual female friend.

- **Bury your gays.** With the rise of nontraditional characters on television shows and movies has also come this disturbing trend: Gay characters far more often meet unceremonious deaths. Lesbians, especially, are killed off at an alarming rate. A subset of this trend is the murder of transgender characters (particularly sex workers) on crime shows. This trope is based on progress (more diversity) but, unfortunately, diverse characters are then treated as more disposable than their heteronormative counterparts.

- **"Sissy" villains.** The evil masterminds are repeatedly played as charming, intelligent, but effeminate villains who love their cats, chess, and classical music. They dress immaculately and surround themselves with beautiful things. Too bad they're also trying to take over the world. They are usually conquered by an extremely masculine (and straight) hero. This trope is as old as action movies themselves.

Education and awareness play a vital role in improving non-binary representation. Media creators, including writers, directors, and producers, should engage in extensive research, consultation, and collaboration with non-binary individuals and communities to ensure accurate and respectful portrayals. This work includes understanding the nuances of gender identity, pronoun usage, and non-binary experiences.

Progress toward inclusiveness continues, and the fight for authentic LGBTQ+ representation is far from over. It requires a continued push for diversity *behind* the camera as well as in front of it, ensuring that LGBTQ+ individuals have a seat at the table when it comes to creating and telling their own stories. It also demands that media institutions and platforms prioritize inclusivity in their programming and actively seek out diverse voices and perspectives.

CONCLUSION

Media has the power to shape societal perceptions and attitudes. By portraying non-binary characters authentically, challenging stereotypes, and fostering inclusivity, media can play a pivotal role in promoting understanding, acceptance, and equality. Non-binary representation in media can create a more inclusive and empathetic society, where individuals of all gender identities can feel seen, heard, and valued.

As we continue to advocate for increased non-binary representation, we can celebrate the progress made thus far while acknowledging the work that still needs to be done. By amplifying non-binary voices, challenging societal norms, and promoting diverse and authentic representations, we open the way for an inclusive and equitable future.

Representing LGBT+ individuals in the media is not just about entertainment but validation, acceptance, and the fight for equality. Authentic and diverse representation can shape societal norms and challenge stereotypes. It is time for the media industry to embrace this responsibility and work towards a future where we see, hear, and celebrate everyone's stories.

As consumers of media, we also have a role to play. We can support and uplift content that provides authentic representation while also holding media accountable for harmful portrayals. We can contribute to a more inclusive media landscape by demanding and supporting accurate and diverse representations.

♥

CHAPTER FIVE:
REAL HOUSEWIVES
AND BEYOND

PORTRAYAL OF WOMEN IN THE MEDIA

The media and entertainment industry significantly shapes our perceptions and ideas about gender roles and equality. It can challenge traditional stereotypes and promote diversity by giving voice to underrepresented groups. We have discussed how the media now works toward providing a voice to non-binary and transgender persons and the tropes that still need to end.

Progress is good, but as a champion of women's equity, I find it dismally remarkable how the women in the media continue struggling to catch up, plagued by systemic sexism, stereotyping, and glass ceiling after glass ceiling.

If women (and by this, throughout this chapter, I mean all people who identify as women) still cannot manage to take a firm and respectable position of equity in the media, how much hope does any underrepresented group have, in the end, of standing on equal ground with the cisgender, Eurocentric male standard?

In fact, there are noticeable discrepancies. Media outlets – advertisers, TV producers, and so on – are taking care right now to promote LGBTQ+ representation because it is a "hot topic" and people take notice. Meanwhile, women's equity drifts to the sidelines where it can be set back lightyears by dozens of reality TV portrayals of "real housewives" and other women as hypersexualized, greedy, vulgar, and catty toward each other, while women's roles in front of and behind the camera, and the world of news and sports broadcasting continue to lag far behind those of men, with inequitable salaries to prove the point.

I am not advocating for *any* underrepresented group to sit on a waiting list for a chance to be treated like human beings. But women are not only half the population on Earth; they comprise a massive sector of the LGBTQ+ community. Equity happens for everyone, or it happens for no one.

Positive gender representation in the media is crucial for several reasons:

- Women make up a significant portion of the audience for film and television, so it is essential to have content that resonates with them and reflects their experiences.

- Diverse storytelling allows a broader range of perspectives and narratives to be shared, enriching the cultural landscape.

- Gender equality in the media industry is a matter of social justice, ensuring women have equal opportunities to succeed and lead in this field.

Research has shown that the portrayal of gender in the media profoundly impacts society. The underrepresentation of women in television has far-reaching consequences. When media denies women equal opportunities to tell their stories and to be seen as leaders, it reinforces societal norms and perpetuates gender inequality. It also limits the aspirations and expectations of young girls, who may not see themselves reflected in the media they consume.

UN-REALITY

When it seems fictional television might progress in gender equity, "reality" steps in like a wrecking ball. Reality television has become a global phenomenon, captivating audiences with its seemingly unscripted and relatable content. However, a closer look reveals that these shows often perpetuate stereotypes and reinforce traditional gender roles. Reality television significantly influences women's portrayals, often perpetuating stereotypes and reinforcing conventional gender roles. These shows rely on simplified characters and scripted narratives to create engaging storylines, but in doing so, they contribute to the marginalization and misrepresentation of certain groups.

Reality television shows have long relied on stereotypes to attract and engage viewers. These stereotypes often depict women in a negative light, reinforcing harmful narratives and perpetuating gender inequalities. According to an article on About.com, reality TV casting agents deliberately select contestants who fit these stereotypes, reducing people to one-dimensional characters to create titillating storylines. This reduction of complex individuals into easily recognizable archetypes distorts reality and reinforces societal biases.

Some common racial and gender stereotypes and tropes include:

The Southern Stereotype: Reality TV takes joy in portraying Southerners as lazy and unintelligent. Shows like *Here Comes Honey Boo Boo* and *Duck Dynasty* often depict families from the South engaging in activities that reinforce these stereotypes. In these shows, the producers seem to make fun of the family rather than authentically portray their lives. Such portrayals not only ridicule the individuals involved but also perpetuate harmful stereotypes about a particular region.

The Italian-American Stereotype: We see another example in the portrayal of Italian-Americans on shows like *Jersey*

Shore. The cast members of this show are often depicted as loud, party-loving individuals with exaggerated behaviors. This portrayal offends many Italian Americans, who feel their culture is being misrepresented and reduced to a caricature. Using derogatory terms and reinforcing negative stereotypes further marginalizes these communities and hinders progress towards equality.

The Husband Hunters: Dating shows like *The Bachelor* have also faced criticism for perpetuating gender stereotypes. These shows often feature a group of women vying for the attention of one man, reinforcing the idea that women obsessively focus on finding a partner and becoming a wife. The emphasis on physical appearance and the exclusion of minorities further exacerbate the problem, conveying that only a specific type of woman is desirable.

White-Privilege Blondes: Youth-directed shows like *The Hills, Laguna Beach,* or *Siesta Key* feature casts of slender, wealthy young women who seem to have nothing more to do than shop, bicker, and betray. These shows feature long lunch-date lineups during which no one eats anything, and the young women discuss problems of "trust" and "honesty." Backstabbing almost inevitably follows, rewarding bad behavior with obsessive attention to the details of tantrums and fights.

Breaking the Fourth Wall: Reality television often employs the fourth wall concept to create drama and tension. When women break the fourth wall and discuss their emotions or physical appearance, they are labeled shallow or attention-seeking. On the other hand, when men break the fourth wall, it is seen as a power move or a strategic decision. This double standard reinforces gender roles and perpetuates the notion that women are overly emotional and self-absorbed.

Relationship nightmares mean fame and ratings. Even though these are real people with, presumably, real emotions at stake, the trashier things get, the better the ratings are for these shows. Most recently we've been victims of the train-wreck of relationships on the Bravo reality series *Vanderpump Rules*. Since early 2023, the "Scandoval" (a play on words from the name of serial cheater, wannabe-actor Tom Sandoval) has dominated gossip headlines, causing viewers to pick sides in a messy, months-long, multiple-party affair centering around the triangle of Tom Sandoval, Ariana Madix and Raquel Leviss.

The drama spawned an incredible number of interviews, special insider shows with cast members, and countless social media firestorms with accompanying hashtags. Viewers could take part actively through social media, showing their support for the different "sides" of the story. Women cast members have been supportive of one another, painfully catty, or down-right violent, but in each case, the audience can't get enough. The show is about to enter its eleventh season. Various parties involved have no trouble using their extra screen time to pro-mote products and sponsors. What seems saddest is the lop-sided fallout. While Sandoval gets to use his angst to appear on a second TV show in addition to (alleged) production cred-its for *Vanderpump Rules* 11th season, "other woman" Raquel (now Rachel) Leviss shares the details of her therapy and apol-ogizes repeatedly for her indiscretions.

MEDIA ANALYSIS AND INTERVENTIONS

It is essential to recognize reality television's power in shap-ing societal perceptions and challenging harmful narratives. Producers and creators of these shows are responsible for con-sidering the consequences of their content and its impact on viewers. Media literacy programs can play a vital role in help-ing individuals critically analyze and understand the messages conveyed by reality television.

Scholars and researchers also emphasize the importance of including a diverse range of reality TV shows in future studies. By examining a wider variety of shows, researchers can gain a deeper understanding of how gender roles and stereotypes are portrayed in reality television.

It is crucial to recognize the power of reality television and work towards creating more inclusive and diverse programming that challenges harmful stereotypes and promotes equality. By promoting media literacy and conducting further research, we can foster a more informed and critical viewership that resists the negative impact of reality television on the portrayal of women.

A study published in *Psychology of Women Quarterly* examined women's portrayals in different reality television genres. The researchers analyzed the content of six shows across four categories: social experiment, subculture, competition, and celebrity programming. The findings revealed no direct relationships between gender portrayals and genre. However, expressive outbursts often interrupted women's behaviors, including emotional displays, violence, and passionate conversational styles. The study also found that women are generally given more screen time than men, which makes it challenging to draw fair conclusions about gender dynamics from reality television. While women may showcase more emotional displays, these occasions are not always frequent, suggesting that not all women fit into the stereotype of being overly emotional.

One individual at the forefront of the fight for gender equality in Hollywood is Oscar-winning actor Geena Davis, founder of the Geena Davis Institute on Gender in Media (its website is seejane.org). Davis recognized the lack of data on the portrayal of women and girls in media and decided to take matters into her own hands. In 2004, she established the institute to conduct in-depth research and collect data on gender representation in film and television.

Davis's institute has played a pivotal role in shedding light on the underrepresentation and misrepresentation of women in the media. Their research uncovered alarming trends, such as the hypersexualization of female characters and the limited dialogue given to women on screen. Their research "examines intersectional onscreen representation of six identities: gender, race, LGBTQIO+, disability, age 50+, and body type," and they have developed some surprising tools to conduct this research, such as the Geena Davis Inclusion Quotient (GD-IQ) and Spellcheck for Bias which analyzes pre-production scripts. With this data, Davis engages with industry stakeholders and raises awareness about the need for change.

Simplifying what the Geena Davis Institute does is not easy, and I invite you to look at seejane.org to get the full impact of their discoveries and recommendations. Their research has revealed significant disparities in the presence and portrayal of women on screen. In children's television, for example, girls are often underrepresented, and when they do appear, they are frequently hypersexualized or given limited dialogue. This limitation not only perpetuates harmful stereotypes but also sends a message to young viewers about the value and role of women in society.

Furthermore, the institute's studies have shown that women are also underrepresented in leading roles in television shows. While there has been progress in recent years, with more female characters taking center stage, there is still a long way to go. In children's films, only around 33% of the leading characters are female, highlighting the persistent gender imbalance in this medium.

A WOMAN'S VOICE: NICOLE RYAN

Nicole Ryan possesses an innate charm and a grounded energy that effortlessly captivates audiences. From her debut as a co-host on *The Morning Mash Up*, a popular daily talk show on SiriusXM Hits 1, she has blossomed into a versatile powerhouse, achieving remarkable success in television, digital media, brand ambassadorship, the live-event industry, and more. Ryan infuses her sharp wit and genuinely radiant presence in all her endeavors.

During *The Morning Mash Up*, Ryan consistently delivers captivating celebrity interviews that are both intriguing and undeniably enjoyable. Her quick thinking and relatable nature are evident in her exceptional interviewing skills, which stem from her underlying philosophy of fostering relaxed and care-free conversations. By creating this atmosphere, Ryan connects with her subjects more deeply.

I enjoyed interviewing Ryan for this book. My research included listening to her thoroughly entertaining podcasts, which often sidetracked me for hours when I should have been writing! I truly appreciate her offering her insights.

Originally from Syracuse, Ryan studied applied psychology at Ithaca College and then moved to New York City shortly after graduation with aspirations of breaking into the marketing side of the entertainment industry.

After securing a temporary receptionist job at Sirius Satellite Radio (a new company in its early stages), Ryan made the most of the opportunity and quickly became the preferred choice for producers who needed voice-over work for promotions and sweepers. This attention led to her appearing on various shows, where her unique female perspective on current issues resonated with audiences. During this time, Ryan realized her aptitude for the fast-paced nature of talk radio. *The Morning Mash Up* soon offered her a co-host position, establishing herself as a formidable female presence in a traditionally male-dominated field.

Ryan advises women looking to break into broadcasting and other industries to keep their eyes open for unexpected chances. "Say yes to as many opportunities as possible. You never know what event or meeting might lead to a new path to further your career. There have been so many things I've forced myself to be part of that I thought would be a waste of time, where I've ended up meeting someone who has changed my life somehow."

Ryan's venture into television has brought her pop-culture insights and sharp comic timing to the forefront. She has made appearances on notable programs such as *Chelsea Lately*, *Good Morning America*, *Guy's Big Bite*, *The Wendy Williams Show*, and *Tamron Hall*.

Her fanbase continues to grow, and in 2018, she launched her digital series through Awestruck, a division of AwesomenessTV. Titled *On-Air Mom* each episode provides an intimate glimpse into Ryan's chronically hectic life as she navigates the challenges of being a working mother in the fast-paced environment of New York City. The series captures all the chaos of juggling a career and raising two young children, offering a refreshingly honest portrayal of family life. In a sea of picture-perfect imagery presented by many mommy bloggers, *On-Air Mom* stands as a much-needed antidote, showcasing the ups and downs of parenthood with candidness and humor.

Ryan maintains her honest and approachable presence on social media, where she regularly shares her experiences as a home cook, fitness enthusiast, and avid reality TV fan. Through her captivating content, she has gained a growing following and is now in high demand as a red-carpet correspondent, keynote speaker, panel moderator, and interviewer at various live events.

Recently, Ryan has expanded her horizons by venturing into podcasting. She co-hosts the exciting new series *Have Kids They Said*, a candid parenting podcast where she joins forces with her former *Mash Up* colleague, Rich Davis. Additionally, she is part of a groundbreaking visual YouTube podcast called *Satisfying*, co-hosting with Sam Roberts.

In each new endeavor, Ryan remains committed to maintaining the genuine and welcoming vibe her loyal fans have come to appreciate. With this impressive resume of achievements, there's no doubt Ryan is a permanent influence on the media. She says, "I'd like to be known for making people smile. I've always considered my job a way to change the world, one person at a time. If I can make someone feel good, loved, or not so alone, then I've done my job. I like to feel accessible. Like the journey I'm on, we're all on, together."

Ryan has a simple – and elegant – solution to improve inclusion in the entertainment industry. She says, "I think it's important to be kind in every instance. People in the industry often have a sense of *'we're better than you.'* We're just normal people in extraordinary positions. When on the air, I treat every guest, listener, or fan like part of our family. The whole *'we're in the cool kids club, and you're not'* is so old school and does nothing to further anyone as a human being. Fostering a community benefits you as an entertainer and the people who follow you."

Ryan's story is important to our topic, not only because she created success for herself in a male-dominated field, but because she did so without "pretending" to be a man or skirting the issues, like that of being a working mom. Ryan uses her reality as a source of connection rather than a crutch. She embraces her gender and makes it a natural part of her success, inviting us to do the same.

THE GLASS CEILING, THE GLASS BOOTH, AND THE GLASS DESK

Women in sports and news media have long faced significant challenges and barriers in pursuing equal representation and recognition. Despite advancements in gender equality in various fields, the sports and news media industry continues to be dominated by men, leaving women marginalized and facing discrimination.

In the early days of sportscasting and newscasting, women faced significant barriers to entry. They were often relegated to junior or support roles, while men occupied the crucial positions of directors and producers. Women's lack of representation and opportunities in these industries perpetuated stereotypes and limited their advancement. The gendered division of labor was deeply ingrained, with women expected to focus on fashion and makeup rather than sports or news.

Despite their challenges, pioneering women began to make their mark in the industry. One such trailblazer was Melissa Ludtke, a former sportswriter for *Sports Illustrated*. In 1978, Ludtke filed a lawsuit against Major League Baseball, challenging the prohibition on female reporters entering team locker rooms. Her victory in the case marked a turning point, establishing the locker room as a workplace and paving the way for female reporters to gain equal access.

While progress does happen, women in sportscasting and newscasting continue to face significant obstacles. The "glass ceiling" metaphor aptly describes the barriers preventing women from advancing to top-level positions. They are often excluded from prominent roles such as play-by-play announcers and color commentators in popular male-dominated sports. This symbolic annihilation perpetuates the invisibility of women in the industry, reinforcing gender biases and limiting their growth opportunities.

The ideal on-air positions in sportscasting, such as play-by-play announcing and color commentary, remain elusive for women. Referred to as the "glass booth," these roles symbolize women's invisibility and limited opportunities in the industry. The prevailing norm of male sportscasters perpetuates the exclusion of women, denying them the chance to showcase their talent and expertise. Despite efforts to diversify sports media, progress remains slow in breaking through this glass ceiling.

The concept of post-feminism, rooted in neoliberalism, has perpetuated double standards and gendered expectations for female sportscasters. Women in the industry face constant scrutiny regarding their skills, knowledge, and appearance. Neoliberalism suggests that gender equality has been achieved, burdening individual women to overcome challenges without acknowledging the systemic barriers they face. This expectation of self-reliance hides inequalities and perpetuates gender biases.

Therefore, it is hard to ignore the Glass Booth's literal counterpart: the Glass Desk, which is the sly way of ensuring viewers can see the shapely legs of women broadcasters in their short skirts. The women who do make it into broadcasting must be youthful, model-pretty, and physically fit, while their male counterparts may age, go gray-headed, gain weight, and wear trousers to work.

Women in sportscasting and newscasting face significant challenges, including gendered harassment both offline and online. They are subjected to derogatory comments, misogyny, and gender-based abuse in their everyday work. Harassment in the workplace contributes to a hostile environment and creates a backlash against women in the industry. The persistence of gender structures and stereotypes perpetuates this mistreatment, highlighting the need for systemic change and cultural transformation.

Women in sports and newscasting often engage in affective labor, managing their emotions to navigate challenges. They learn to develop a "thick skin" to endure gender criticism and mistreatment. However, this emotional labor reinforces the industry's masculine norm and maintains women's subordination. The expectation for women to regulate their emotions further highlights the unequal power dynamics and the need for a more inclusive and supportive work environment.

To address the gender disparities in sportscasting and newscasting, it is crucial to promote diversity and inclusion within the industry. Major broadcasters should actively hire women for top-level positions and provide equal opportunities for growth and advancement. Additionally, new broadcasting positions within women's sports should be filled by female journalists, allowing them to gain recognition and challenge traditional gender roles.

Raising awareness about women's challenges in the industry is essential for driving change. By challenging stereotypes and highlighting the competence and expertise of female sportscasters and newscasters, we can shift the narrative and break down gender biases. Providing platforms for women to share their experiences and successes will foster a more inclusive and accepting environment.

If women continue to face challenges, what of transgender and non-binary persons? Only in the past two years have an extremely limited number of anchors announced their status. A mere handful have publicly acknowledged being transgender or non-binary, and such announcements are always met with controversy and fervor. There may be many more people in the public eye who simply say nothing, fearing loss of work or even physical danger. "Coming out," even in countries where transgender rights are decreed by law, is not a guarantee of safety, as was the case for Pakistani transgender news anchor Marvia Malik, who was attacked by gunmen outside her home. Such an event is where public opinion and law come head-to-head.

THE POWER OF MEDIA TO DRIVE CHANGE

Media organizations themselves play a crucial role in promoting gender equity in television. These organizations must prioritize diversity and inclusion in their content and decision-making processes, not only in the portrayal of women on screen but also in the representation of women in leadership positions behind the scenes.

Creating a safe and inclusive work environment is also

vital, as violence and harassment against female media workers remain significant concerns. The industry must address these issues and develop policies and support mechanisms to ensure the safety and well-being of all staff members.

Despite the challenges, there have been positive developments in recent years. More women are speaking out and demanding change, and the industry is starting to respond. The *#MeToo* and *#Time's Up* movements have brought issues of gender inequality to the forefront, leading to increased accountability and a push for greater representation and diversity in all aspects of media.

Media organizations can challenge traditional norms and promote equality by creating gender-sensitive and gender-transformative content. Such content means breaking stereotypes, featuring women in leadership roles, and providing a platform for viewers to see and hear diverse perspectives.

USING HER VOICE FOR CHANGE: NYDIA HAN

At the National Association of Women Business Owners gala last year, I had the opportunity to hear Philadelphia news anchor and journalist, Nydia Han, speak about launching her award-winning 6abc docuseries, *#This is America*. With this series, Nydia wishes to inspire us all to understand our unique American stories, learn to check our own biases, and become agents for change and unity.[3]

Nydia, who is proudly part of the Asian American community, is well-aware of the feeling of "otherness" experienced by those who seem different. She graciously agreed to be interviewed for this book, as a woman who uses her voice to promote diversity, equity and inclusion in the United States, speaking out powerfully against Anti-Asian hate.

Despite being born and raised in Southern California,

---

3   https://www.nydiahan.com/about

Nydia has frequently been asked if she speaks English, or has been complimented on her English-speaking skills. Nydia admits that in her small hometown, few people looked like her – and after college at Northwestern University, and in subsequent reporting jobs in places like Idaho and Oklahoma City, which had small Asian-American populations, she was almost always "the other."

In 2017, Nydia was subjected to ignorance that shocked her into devoted action. Han recounted, "As I was walking, a driver made a turn and almost hit me. We exchanged words about who had the right of way, and as the person drove off, she shouted, 'This is America!'"

That remark left Nydia reeling. She assumed the driver said those words to her because the driver did not see her as an American. Nydia could only be thankful that her children were not there to witness the incident, which she would have been at a loss to explain to them.

A few days later, still feeling the sting of that phrase, "This is America," Nydia recorded a Facebook Live Video in response to the driver. The fiery video went viral as Nydia let out all the hurt she felt, not only for that incident but for all the times she had ever been treated as not belonging because of her appearance. She showed herself as a proud Asian American woman. The video received over three million views and over 16,000 comments – most positive, though not all. Not wishing to leave the conversation there, Nydia embarked on her docuseries #*This is America* and a TedX talk.

Nydia has this to say about her experience working on the docuseries. "I was able to put my investigative journalist hat back on and meet with a few of the individuals who left a dissenting or critical comment on the video. I went out into the community and met them at their homes, and asked to have an open and honest conversation. I realized, during those talks, that it opened up space to understand what we have in common so that we could have a respectful conversation about our differences. Unfamiliarity breeds fear and fear breeds hate. We have to approach each other with curiosity to find understanding and love."

Nydia wants all communities to feel seen and heard, and to be informed of their histories and the histories of others. She says, "I hope that will open our collective lens to try to understand and see diverse American experiences." To that end, as a news anchor, she regularly talks about her perspectives as an Asian American and a woman of Korean descent on the air. The advice she gives to students wishing to break into the media is, "It is important to have diversity in the newsroom. It is about telling other people's stories, but also bringing your full self to work to connect with your audience."

CONCLUSION

Exposure to gendered stereotypes in the media can influence children's preferences, perceptions of gender roles, and expectations for their future. When girls do not see empowered and diverse female characters on screen, it can impact their self-esteem and limit their belief in what they can achieve. On the other hand, when boys are predominantly exposed to male characters in positions of power and authority, it can reinforce gender biases and perpetuate inequity.

Children are affected by the gendered stereotypes presented to them from a young age through various media forms. These stereotypes can shape their preferences, perceptions of gender roles, and expectations for their future trajectories in life. It is, therefore, crucial to challenge these stereotypes and provide more diverse and empowering representations of women on screen.

Challenges, discrimination, and limited opportunities have marked the journey for women in sportscasting and newscasting. The gender disparities and double standards they face are deeply rooted in societal constructs and biases. However, progress has been made through the resilience and determination of trailblazing women. By advocating for equality, challenging stereotypes, and promoting diversity and inclusion, we can create a more equitable future for women in the industry.

Empowering the next generation of women in entertainment, sportscasting, and newscasting is crucial for creating lasting change. By encouraging girls and young women to pursue careers in media through seminars, workshops, and mentorship programs, we can inspire future generations to challenge societal norms and strive for equality. Education and exposure to diverse role models will help dismantle barriers and create a more inclusive industry.

We will see that as equity is achieved for women, equity for intersections of other underrepresented groups will improve because, logically, it must. No, it will not happen overnight or without controversy. Let's look at the social and legal changes happening worldwide as we endeavor to recognize humanity with all its faces.

♥

CHAPTER SIX:
SPORTS AND GENDER

Sports have always been a powerful force that brings people together, transcending cultural, social, and economic boundaries. They can unite individuals from different backgrounds, cultures, and beliefs, creating a sense of community and shared passion. However, while sports have the potential to promote diversity and inclusion, they can also highlight and amplify differences. Diversity in sports has become increasingly important in recent years.

Yet the question of "diversity" in sports has historically been targeted toward racial, or perhaps cultural, diversity. Gender diversity is new on the playing field and more complicated by our contemporary understanding of gender beyond men and women. Cisgender women remain embroiled in their battle for sports equity, and transgender/nonbinary sports equity is not just a philosophical question but a literal legal battle across the United States.

In recent years, there has been a growing global debate surrounding the inclusion of transgender and nonbinary athletes in sports. While LGBTQ+ rights campaigners argue for equal opportunities and inclusivity, opponents claim that transgender women have unfair physical advantages over cisgender women.

This controversy has led to the introduction of various regulations by sports organizations and state legislatures, with some imposing restrictions on the participation of transgender athletes. However, it is essential to challenge the misconceptions surrounding this issue and promote a more inclusive and accepting environment for all athletes, regardless of their gender identity.

UNIVERSAL INCLUSION: MAGALI ROY

Magali Roy provided me with direct insight into the role that the NHL organization has played in her life as the wife of Ian Laperrière, a star player turned Philadelphia coach.

That she and Laperrière were high school sweethearts in Montreal, Canada, is a well-known and much-beloved facet of this pair. After meeting as teenagers, they embarked on a long-distance relationship that spanned two different countries for multiple years. While they saw each other a few times during the season and the summer, Roy completed her pharmacy degree while Ian focused on his sports career.

In 1997, Roy immigrated to the United States. As a French-Canadian woman, adapting to the language and culture in the States was a thrilling challenge that Roy embraced wholeheartedly. Los Angeles became her new home. In 1999, she and Ian tied the knot. Their son Tristan arrived in 2002, followed by Zach in 2004.

In 2011, they proudly became citizens of the United States in Mount Laurel, New Jersey.

Moving to Philadelphia was a far cry from the sunny streets of LA, but the city's undeniable charm captivated Roy. Her husband was excited for the chance to retire here with the hopes of eventually coaching. Her boys fell head over heels for the Philly area, too – they loved walking to school and forging lifelong friendships.

It took a bit of time for Roy to acclimate fully, but there was no turning back once she did. She found her place and started giving back to the community that embraced her family openly.

Roy and Laperrière's family has had a strong, positive

impact on the Philadelphia community. Roy takes immense pride in her charity work through the team's charity organization, especially with the Philadelphia area's children in need.

Roy has nothing but good things to say about the inclusion she felt from the NHL community. As the spouse of a 16-season NHL player, Roy often had to manage things at home by herself. She knows the value of being surrounded by the right kind of support. She has had the privilege of being part of a fantastic community that embraces and supports one another. Whether cheering on the team from the stands or mingling in the locker room, the spouses and families always feel welcome. The NHL has genuinely been a pillar in her life.

One of the most rewarding aspects has been the opportunity for players' families to come together. From engaging in activities for the wives, children, and loved ones to celebrating special moments like birthdays and holidays with their hockey family, they built lifelong connections beyond the rink. Roy always felt in the right place despite the challenges of leaving ties behind and forming new ones. "I want to be remembered as fully grounded," says Roy. "and that I was always there to support Ian."

Her advice echoes what I heard from my other interviews: that we achieve inclusion on a personal level as well as a corporate and societal level. She reminds us of the importance of staying grounded and accepting offered support. Her words also emphasize the importance of organizations in creating environments where people feel welcomed, safe, and accepted.

GOING BACK: WOMEN'S INCLUSION IN SPORTS

Sports have long been a platform for human achievement, showcasing the extraordinary physical and mental capabilities of athletes. Throughout history, women faced significant challenges and discrimination in the world of sports. From ancient civilizations to the modern era, the journey of women in sports has been a relentless battle for recognition, equality, and acceptance.

Although, contrary to popular belief, women's participation in sports is not a recent phenomenon. Even in ancient civilizations, some women defied societal norms and engaged in athletic pursuits. In Homer's *Odyssey*, Princess Nausicaa and her handmaidens are depicted playing ball on a riverbank, showcasing women's involvement in sports.

In Ancient Greece, although women were restricted from participating in most Olympic events, they could compete in foot races at festivals. Equestrian events also provided an avenue for women to achieve Olympic victories. Spartan women, known for their fierce warrior culture, participated in sports on par with men, engaging in wrestling, javelin throwing, foot racing, and discus events. Similarly, certain African tribes, such as the Key Faduy tribe in the south-central Sahara, celebrated female power through ritual competitions and wrestling arts.

The Victorian era in Western European cultures brought about a period of immense sexism and societal restrictions for women. The ideal Victorian woman was expected to be gentle and frail, with strenuous physical activity strongly discouraged. Myths and misconceptions surrounding women's participation in sports included beliefs that it could harm their reproductive organs or deplete their energy, leading to weak offspring.

Despite these limitations, informal athletic clubs emerged in the late 1800s and early 1900s, providing women with opportunities to engage in sports. The 1900 Olympics witnessed the participation of 22 women in events such as sailing, croquet, and equestrian sports. Tennis and lawn golf were designated as women-only events. In 1922, the first Women's Olympic Games took place in Paris, featuring physically demanding events like shot put and the 1000-meter dash.

Title IX: A Turning Point for Gender Equality

The passage of Title IX of the Education Amendments Act in 1972 marked a significant turning point for gender equality in sports. This landmark legislation aimed to eliminate sex discrimination in federally funded education programs, including athletics. Prior to Title IX, women had limited opportunities in sports, with fewer than 30,000 collegiate athletes in the United States.

Title IX revolutionized women's participation in sports, leading to a substantial increase in opportunities at both the high school and collegiate levels. By 2012, the number of girls participating in high school sports in the U.S. had risen tenfold, surpassing three million. Moreover, over 190,000 women competed in intercollegiate sports, six times more than in 1972.

Despite undeniable progress, women in sports still face numerous challenges and controversies:

- Gender confirmation exams and mandatory tests for high testosterone levels have been imposed on female athletes, raising concerns about fairness and discrimination.

- Pay inequity in sports has also been a persistent issue, with female athletes earning lower wages and prize money compared to their male counterparts.

- Research in sports psychology, a crucial field for athlete performance, has predominantly focused on male participants. Studies between 2010 and 2020 revealed that 62% of participants in sport psychology research were men and boys. This gender imbalance limits our understanding of how women experience sports and hampers the development of tailored strategies for their peak performance.

Despite the challenges, women athletes and advocates continue to fight for equality in sports. Increased media coverage, public interest, and improved opportunities are contributing to the growth of women's sports. Female athletes like Serena Williams, Simone Biles, and Megan Rapinoe are breaking barriers and inspiring future generations.

Efforts to address gender bias in research and ensure equal representation are crucial. Researchers and funding bodies must strive to develop an evidence base that accurately represents the experiences and needs of women in sports.

As we look toward the future, we must continue championing gender equity in sports. Doing so requires dismantling long-standing biases, conducting inclusive research, advocating for fair treatment, and providing equal opportunities for all athletes and their families.

Another prominent example, Kylie Kelce, the wife of NFL star Jason Kelce and breakout star of the Kelce documentary released on Prime, is actively reshaping the traditional perception of WAGs (wives and girlfriends) in the world of sports. Unlike the stereotypical portrayal of WAGs solely as glamorous figures on the sidelines, Kylie is emerging as a multifaceted influencer and businesswoman in her own right. With a strong presence on social media platforms like Instagram, she utilizes her platform to showcase her vibrant personality, sports skills in her own right, entrepreneurial endeavors, and philanthropic initiatives. By sharing insights into her life beyond the confines of being a football player's wife, Kylie is challenging the narrow stereotypes often associated with WAGs, demonstrating that they are individuals with their own aspirations, passions, and achievements.

Moreover, Kylie Kelce's impact extends beyond the realm of sports, as she actively engages with her community and advocates for important social causes. Through her involvement in various charitable organizations and initiatives, she leverages her platform to raise awareness and drive positive change on issues ranging from women's empowerment to autism support and awareness. By using her influence for social good and promoting authenticity, inclusivity, and empowerment, Kylie is not only changing the perception of WAGs but also inspiring others to embrace their individuality and make a meaningful impact in their own spheres of influence.

Even with the numerous examples of strong female presence in the sports world, once more, we find ourselves in the dilemma of a paradigm shift. If women athletes/family members are still unable to find equity in sports, what happens when we introduce transgender or nonbinary athletes?

CONTROVERSY SURROUNDING TRANSGENDER ATHLETES

In recent years, several states have passed or proposed legislation to restrict transgender youth's participation in sports. For example, Idaho became the first state to pass a law banning transgender student-athletes from playing sports consistent with their gender identity. Similar laws have been introduced in many other states, with varying degrees of success. The proposed federal legislation, H.R. 734, seeks to amend Title IX to define sex based solely on reproductive biology and genetics at birth, effectively excluding transgender women and girls from participating in female sports teams.

These discriminatory policies have a significant impact on transgender athletes, particularly transgender girls. The bans deny them the opportunity to compete alongside their peers and can have detrimental effects on their mental health and well-being. Transgender athletes often face disproportionate levels of harassment and discrimination, and these bans further marginalize and stigmatize them. It is essential to recognize that transgender athletes, like their cisgender counterparts, have a right to participate in sports and enjoy the benefits it brings.

Let's look at the problems facing inclusion.

The Argument Against Inclusion

Critics of transgender inclusion in sports often argue that trans women have an unfair advantage due to the physiological effects of male puberty, such as increased muscle mass and bone density. Prominent figures, including tennis champion Martina Navratilova and marathon runner Paula Radcliffe, have expressed concerns about the alleged advantage that trans women may have over cisgender women.

The Perspective of LGBTQ+ Activists and Athletes

LGBTQ+ activists have long advocated for the inclusion of transgender athletes, highlighting the discriminatory nature of bans and restrictions. They argue that such measures perpetuate a climate of hostility towards the trans community and hinder their participation in sports at all levels. Organizations like Mermaids, a British charity supporting trans youth, emphasize that no young person should have to choose between being their authentic selves and participating in the sports they love.

Sports Authorities' Policies and Guidelines

Various sports bodies and organizations have implemented rules and regulations concerning the participation of transgender athletes. The Union Cycliste Internationale (UCI), for instance, recently banned transgender female athletes from competing in women's events if they transitioned after puberty. Similarly, Swim England, World Athletics, Scottish Rugby, FINA, England's Rugby Football Union, and the International

Rugby League have enforced restrictions on trans women who transitioned after puberty. The International Olympic Committee (IOC) revised its guidelines, allowing individual sports to determine the eligibility of trans athletes.

However, these controversies neglect to make some critical considerations:

- The diverse experiences and abilities within the transgender community.

- Recognizing the transgender community members' right to compete and thrive in their chosen sports.

- Policies are often not based on scientific evidence but on stereotypes and discrimination.

DEBUNKING MYTHS ABOUT TRANSGENDER ATHLETES

To foster a more inclusive and informed discussion, we must address and debunk common myths surrounding transgender athletes. By challenging these misconceptions, we can promote a more empathetic and understanding approach to transgender inclusion in sports.

Myth 1: Trans Athletes Have an Unfair Advantage

One prevalent myth is that transgender athletes inherently possess physical advantages over cisgender athletes. However, it is crucial to recognize the diversity of athletic abilities within both the transgender and cisgender communities. Just as cisgender athletes vary in their athletic prowess, so do transgender athletes. Factors such as technique, training, and dedication play significant roles in an athlete's performance, regardless of their gender identity. Experts, such as Dr. Joshua D. Safer, emphasize that there is no inherent reason to treat the physiological characteristics of transgender women differently from those of cisgender women.

Myth 2: Transgender Girls Are Not "Real" Girls

Another harmful myth perpetuated by opponents of transgender inclusion is the notion that transgender girls are not "real" girls. This assertion denies the validity of transgender individuals' gender identities and undermines their rights to participate in sports aligned with their gender identity. It is essential to recognize that biological characteristics do not solely determine gender. Gender also encompasses a person's deeply held sense of self. Transgender girls are girls, and they deserve the same opportunities to participate in sports as cisgender girls.

Myth 3: Trans Students Require Separate Teams

Opponents of transgender inclusion often argue for the creation of separate teams for transgender athletes. However, this approach perpetuates segregation and discrimination, further marginalizing transgender individuals. Inclusive sports environments benefit all students by fostering team unity, promoting non-discrimination, and providing valuable social and emotional support. Excluding transgender students from athletics sends a harmful message that they are outsiders and reinforces social stigmatization.

Myth 4: Inclusion of Trans Athletes Hurts Cisgender Women

A common argument against the inclusion of transgender athletes is that it harms cisgender women. However, this perspective fails to recognize the complexity of gender and perpetuates harmful stereotypes. Excluding transgender women from women's sports invites invasive gender policing and reinforces the notion that women are weak and in need of protection. In reality, the inclusion of transgender athletes promotes non-discrimination and unity among all student-athletes, benefiting cisgender women as well.

WINDMILLS

As we review this controversy and its resulting problematic legislation, as well as the possible solutions, keep this puzzle in mind: By far, the majority of the controversy's focus is on whether transgender women or girls should participate in women's sports, with the main fear being that since they are biologically male, these individuals will have a physical advantage over their competitors.

Finding information regarding transgender men striving to compete in men's sports is actually quite tricky; nobody seems particularly worried that a woman who has a gender-affirming surgery will overtake football and put the men athletes out of their jobs. Do I have an answer for this double standard? Not really. Merely a hypothesis: men's sports are not worried about transgender athletes because that is a diversity issue, and therefore, it is lumped in where all gender diversity issues seem to fall: alongside "women's issues." This sleight-of-hand is why women should support transgender and nonbinary rights in sports under all circumstances: because they are all treated with the same general dismissiveness by the powerhouse that is men's sports. Does anyone else get the feeling that women and nonbinary people are given windmills to fight instead of actual dragons?

THE IMPORTANCE OF INCLUSIVE POLICIES AND PRACTICES

Windmills or not, we must begin somewhere. Creating an inclusive and accepting environment for transgender and nonbinary athletes requires the implementation of comprehensive policies and practices.

Diversity in sports goes beyond just representation; it encompasses the inclusion of individuals from various cultural backgrounds, races, ethnicities, genders, sexual orientations, religions, and abilities while creating an environment that celebrates and values these differences, allowing everyone to participate, compete, and succeed on an equal footing.

Sports organizations, state legislatures, and educational institutions should prioritize inclusivity and challenge discriminatory measures. By embracing diversity and promoting equality, we can ensure that all athletes, regardless of their gender identity, have the opportunity to participate and excel in sports. Here are some ways we can begin:

Educating coaches, officials, and administrators. To foster inclusivity, we should provide education and training to coaches, officials, and administrators involved in youth and professional sports. These stakeholders are vital in creating an inclusive and supportive environment for transgender and nonbinary athletes.

Implementing inclusive policies and guidelines. Sports organizations, state legislatures, and educational institutions should adopt trans-inclusive policies and procedures that prioritize the rights and well-being of transgender and nonbinary athletes. These policies should be based on scientific evidence, promote fairness, and challenge stereotypes. By establishing clear guidelines for eligibility and participation, we can create an inclusive framework that upholds the principles of equality and non-discrimination. Sports organizations and policymakers should work towards breaking down barriers to participation for individuals from diverse backgrounds. They can do so by providing accessible facilities, addressing financial barriers, and implementing policies that promote equal opportunities for all. By removing these barriers, more individuals can have the chance to participate and excel in sports.

Supporting transgender athletes' mental and emotional well-being. Transgender athletes often face significant challenges, including discrimination, marginalization, and mental health issues. It is crucial to provide supportive resources, such as counseling services and LGBTQ+-inclusive support networks, to address the unique needs of transgender athletes. By prioritizing their mental and emotional well-being, we can create an environment where transgender athletes can thrive and excel in their chosen sports.

Promoting representation and visibility. Representation and visibility play a crucial role in challenging societal norms and promoting acceptance of transgender and nonbinary athletes. By showcasing the accomplishments and stories of transgender athletes at all levels of sports, we can challenge stereotypes and inspire future generations. Media outlets, sports organizations, and sponsors should actively seek opportunities to elevate the voices and experiences of transgender athletes, promoting a more inclusive and diverse sporting landscape.

Shaping exercise and sports participation. Cultural factors play a significant role in shaping training and sports participation. Different cultures have unique sporting traditions, preferences, and approaches to physical activity. Understanding these cultural nuances is crucial in designing sports programs that cater to diverse communities. By incorporating cultural elements and adapting sports to suit different cultural contexts, the sport becomes more inclusive and appeals to a wider range of individuals.

Enforcing equity in media representation. We have already discussed this at length: as a society, we believe what the media tells us. Media plays an influential role in shaping cultural perceptions of sports, athletes, and coaches. The way the media portrays diverse cultures can either reinforce stereotypes or challenge them. Media representations must be fair, accurate, and inclusive, allowing diverse voices and stories to be heard. As always, acceptance and exposure can help break down cultural barriers, promote understanding, and foster a more inclusive sports culture.

Engaging in mentorship and support. Creating mentorship and support programs can be instrumental in promoting cultural diversity in sports. By pairing athletes and coaches from diverse backgrounds with experienced mentors, they can receive guidance, support, and opportunities for growth. This can help address the underrepresentation of diverse cultures in leadership positions and create a more inclusive sports environment.

Engaging in collaboration and partnerships. Collaboration and partnerships between sports organizations, community organizations, and cultural groups are essential for promoting cultural diversity in sports. By working together, they can develop programs and initiatives that celebrate diversity, foster inclusion, and provide opportunities for diverse individuals to participate and excel in sports.

MEN'S SPORTS, WOMEN'S SPORTS, AND THE NONBINARY

Binary trans people (trans women and trans men) are the most visible players in the fight for inclusion. But nonbinary athletes, who do not identify with either gender, have often been left out of the conversation.

They are making themselves known. Dealing equitably with athletes who identify as two or more genders, no gender, or another gender besides man or woman, requires a shift in how we currently categorize athletics into the two fairly distinct categories of men's and women's sports.

Many nonbinary athletes have made themselves known and become representatives for the cause of inclusion: Layshia Clarendon is the first WNBA player to be openly nonbinary; pairs figure-skater Timothy LeDuc was the first openly nonbinary athlete to qualify for the Winter Olympics, while skateboarder Alana Smith was the first nonbinary Summer Olympics participant. In the Paralympics, athletes like wheelchair racer Robyn Lambird have come out as nonbinary. These are but a few pioneers who represent nonbinary athletes, promoting change by example.

We can expect the number of openly nonbinary athletes to increase as inclusion progresses. Perhaps the solution lies in taking gender out of the equation entirely – there are no longer "men's sports" or "women's sports," but simply sports. There are no longer men or women athletes, but simply athletes. A dividing line between competitors must become something that is reliably nonbiased if a dividing line must exist at all.

THE GROWING BACKLASH AND RECENT LEGISLATION

In March 2023, World Athletics, the governing body for track and field events, introduced a ban on transgender women who had gone through male puberty from participating in elite female competitions. This decision was made in an effort to protect the integrity of the female category.

Sebastian Coe, the president of World Athletics, emphasized the necessity of implementing these rules. He stated that the overarching need to protect the female category was the driving force behind the decision. This move by World Athletics set a precedent for other sports organizations to reevaluate their own eligibility criteria.

World Aquatics, the governing body for aquatic sports, followed in the footsteps of World Athletics by implementing similar eligibility restrictions in 2022. This decision meant that transgender women who had undergone male puberty would no longer be able to compete in the female category. Instead, they would have the option to participate in the newly created "men/open" category.

The International Cycling Union (UCI) joined the movement in July 2023 by banning transgender women who had undergone male puberty from competing in the female category of competitive events. This decision aligned with British Cycling's earlier ban on transgender women. These bans have had a significant impact on athletes like Laurel Hubbard, who previously met the testosterone level requirements to compete in the women's category.[4]

Transgender athletes, along with their allies and supporters, argue that transgender women should have the right to compete in the category that aligns with their gender identity. They emphasize the importance of inclusivity and affirming the identities of transgender individuals.

Halba Diouf, a French sprinter, expressed frustration with the tightening of eligibility rules, stating, "The only safeguard transgender women have is their right to live as they wish, and we are being refused that, we are being hounded." These sentiments reflect the struggle faced by transgender individuals who feel marginalized and denied opportunities in sports.[5]

On the other side of the debate, critics, including some anti-trans activists, argue that the participation of transgender women poses a threat to the integrity of women's sports. They raise concerns about potential advantages that transgender women may have due to physiological differences developed during male puberty.

The inclusion of high-profile transgender athletes like Lia Thomas, a swimmer who became the first openly transgender athlete to win an NCAA Division 1 US national college title, has intensified these concerns. Thomas, despite her accomplishments, is now unable to compete in the women's category at the Paris Olympics due to the new rules set by World Aquatics.

The discussion surrounding transgender athletes has drawn

------

4 https://www.nbcnews.com/nbc-out/out-news/pendulum-swings-tighter-measures-transgender-athletes-rcna131461

5 Ibid.

opinions from some of the world's most prominent athletes. Megan Rapinoe, a retired member of the US women's soccer team, voiced her support for transgender inclusion, stating that she would welcome a transgender player on the squad. Rapinoe emphasized the need to protect the full humanity of individuals and criticized the weaponization of women's sports.[6] Rapinoe's comments sparked a broader conversation about the complexities of balancing fairness and inclusivity in sports.

CONCLUSION

Cultural diversity in sports is not only essential for promoting inclusivity and representation but also for fostering a more understanding and accepting society. By embracing diversity, breaking down barriers, and promoting inclusion, sports can become a powerful force for positive change. It is the responsibility of sports organizations, policymakers, athletes, coaches, and the broader community to work together toward creating a sports culture that celebrates and values the richness of our diverse world.

Remember, sports can unite us all, regardless of our cultural backgrounds. As the sporting world opens its doors to all, we'll forge a path because we'll all be moving in the same direction. Sports leagues must adapt and evolve to accommodate their players or put the whole boundary-defying spirit of sports at risk.

---

6 Ibid.

♥

CHAPTER SEVEN:
JUSTINE LINDSAY, A TRAILBLAZING CHEERLEADER

The all-American image of a cheerleader may be one of the most heteronormative "girl" icons we know. That's why it was such a delight to have the chance to speak to Justine Lindsay, who is known in the media for being the NFL's first openly transgender cheerleader.

That's a significant role to fill in the LGBTQ+ movement and one that could overwhelm someone without a good head on their shoulders, a solid foundation of faith and self-confidence, and a refusal to stoop to the level of those who disparage her. I found Justine humble, charming, funny, and incredibly down-to-earth. Her inspiring journey from a dance enthusiast to a member of a prestigious cheerleading squad made history. It ignited conversations about inclusivity and acceptance in the traditionally conservative realm of professional sports.

Justine is from Charlotte, North Carolina, where her single mother raised her. She describes her childhood as sheltered; she grew up in a safe, middle-class environment with protective older siblings and a strong relationship with her mom. She remembers always being in church, singing in the gospel choir. Though her parents were separated, she saw her father regularly on the weekends.

Justine Lindsay's love for dance blossomed when she was only five, and she was mesmerized by a performance of "Revelations." The art form spoke to her soul. With the support and encouragement of her mother, she embarked on ballet lessons that would lay the foundation for her future achievements.

Lindsay didn't grow up around the LGBTQ+ community. She had no exposure to others who felt uncomfortable with their birth-assigned gender. "I knew when I was growing up that I was ... not different – but special."

Lindsay's talent and dedication soon caught the attention of renowned institutions. By the time she was 14, she was accepted for a full scholarship to the Debbie Allen Dance Academy in Los Angeles with 100 other young dancers.

She went alone, leaving the sanctuary of her close-knit family to live with a host family in LA; there, she attended her first and second year of high school and trained in dancing each day from 3:00 p.m. to 10:00 p.m. Luckily, Lindsay lived with a warm, welcoming host family. Though being away from her mother was difficult, she formed a great relationship with her host mother. When Justine returned to Charlotte, she was permitted to skip straight to her senior year and graduate early.

Between high school and college, Lindsay began exploring who she really was. After she started taking hormones, the mental and physical changes were a complete turnaround. Lindsay reflects, "I was shocked by how my body changed but appreciative of that change." She received incredible support from her family during this time.

When the opportunity to audition for the cheerleading squad arose, Lindsay hesitated momentarily. Her break from dancing had gone on for almost eight years. She discovered, however, that "Once you've got it, you've got it," when it came to dance – plus, she had always wanted to be a cheerleader. Driven by her determination to prove doubters wrong and shatter stereotypes while following a long-held dream, she embraced the challenge wholeheartedly.

The grueling audition process pitted her against hundreds of hopefuls, all vying for a coveted spot on the team. Lindsay's talent, charisma, and unwavering spirit propelled her to success, securing her place as the first transgender cheerleader to don the uniform.

The journey has not been without its fair share of challenges. Lindsay has faced a barrage of negative comments and bigotry on social media.

"There are trolls out there," Lindsay told me. "I try not to let it affect me; I don't want to feed into it. Trolls will try to use God and religion against me. But God grounds me at all times. I am a humble individual who loves to dance and entertain. I hope I can be an inspiration, a 'big sister.'"

A common misunderstanding that comes Lindsay's way is that she somehow "took" a cheerleading spot from a woman. But this is untrue, especially considering the diversity promoted by her organization. "I did not take a woman's place on the cheerleading team. We have male cheerleaders on the team."

In fact, Lindsay has publicly expressed her gratitude towards her fellow cheerleaders, Melvin Sutton, Tre Booker, and Chris Crawford, who made history themselves as the first three men to become cheerleaders. Their support and camaraderie played a pivotal role in her journey, breaking down barriers and challenging preconceived notions about gender roles in cheerleading. Their collective presence on the team showcases their individual talents and demonstrates the power of diversity and inclusion in the sports industry.

Lindsay remains resilient, focusing on the positive support and encouragement she has received from within the organization, her teammates, her coach, and the Charlotte community. This unwavering support has fortified Lindsay's resolve to strongly advocate for her community and inspire young transgender individuals to embrace their true selves.

For Justine Lindsay, being part of the squad is about more than just cheerleading; it is about becoming a face of possibility and empowerment. Lindsay's presence on the field represents a significant milestone in the journey towards inclusivity and acceptance. By challenging societal norms and breaking down barriers, she sends a powerful message to young trans individuals that they, too, can pursue their dreams and overcome obstacles. But as for her role as a trailblazer, Lindsay claims that's not her impression of the situation: she stepped into herself rather than blazing a new trial. "I've been dancing since I was five. I don't feel like a trailblazer. It's second nature to me."

Justine Lindsay's journey as the first openly transgender cheerleader in the NFL is a testament to the power of resilience, determination, and the ability to break down barriers. Her love for dance and her unwavering spirit led her to achieve extraordinary milestones. Performing her dream job as a cheerleader is "a blessing, but a humbling experience."

"I get negativity from people who don't know me or my story. But I get a lot of support from teammates and the LGBTQ+ community."

I asked Lindsay what advice she would give to transgender youth interested in a profession in sports or sports media. "Before anything, do your research," she recommended. "Never put yourself in a situation where you are politicalized. Make sure it's something you are passionate about. Stay being yourself – don't let others mold you. Be you the way you need to be you. And as long as you are happy, keep grinding and push forward."

She also adds, "Patience is key. You have to play the game."

Lindsay has engaged in a great deal of public speaking regarding gender inclusivity in sports and how members of the sporting world could foster a more inclusive environment. She feels inclusivity must start in schools and then be nurtured through conversation. The quest is to make everyone feel welcome. "You can't say you support LGBTQ+ while still having LBGTQ+ individuals on the team who are uncomfortable at being out."

These days, Lindsay is content to remain in Charlotte, where she intends to continue breaking ground and creating conversations about transgender inclusivity in sports. Someday, she plans to return to Los Angeles. A podcaster and digital creator, in addition to being a cheerleader, Lindsay envisions herself becoming someone like Wendy Williams with her own playful, funny spin. She hopes her name will become a household word!

As to her legacy, Lindsay hopes that she can help "change the narrative of how trans women are viewed. We are moms, NFL cheerleaders, actresses, lawyers, doctors. I want to inspire people by being a regular human who worked hard and made her way."

♥

CHAPTER EIGHT: TOUCHDOWN FOR EQUITY

JALEN HURTS' ALL-FEMALE MANAGEMENT TEAM

Current Philadelphia Eagles quarterback Jalen Hurts is rewriting the record books on the field and making history off the field. He assembled an all-female management team, reshaping the landscape of sports representation. Led by his agent, Nicole Lynn, this groundbreaking team is not only shattering glass ceilings but also proving that women can excel in traditionally male-dominated industries.[7]

Jalen Hurts burst onto the scene with his exceptional play at the college level. His success caught the attention of NFL scouts, and in the 2020 NFL Draft, he was selected by the Philadelphia Eagles in the second round.

Nicole Lynn, the quarterback's agent and a trailblazer in the sports industry, is at the forefront of Jalen Hurts' all-female management team. Lynn is the President of Football at Klutch Sports; Chantal Romain, Shakeemah Simmons-Winter, and Jenna Malphrus work for Klutch. Joe D'Amelio is Head of Football Marketing at Klutch Sports and has also contributed to Jalen's off the field endeavors.

Lynn had already represented several notable athletes, including Quinnen Williams, before she crossed paths with Jalen Hurts. Lynn's impressive track record of representing top

---

7 https://www.womensleadershiptoday.com/initiative-and-determination-nicole-lynn-jalen-hursts-all-woman-team/ and https://insidetheiggles.com/2023/02/03/jalen-hurts-female-management-team/

athletes and her unwavering dedication to her clients earned her a reputation as one of the most respected agents in the business. Her determination and passion for her work caught Hurts' attention, and after a meeting to discuss their potential partnership, it became clear to both parties that they were the perfect match.

In April 2023, Lynn and her team were key in getting Hurts a $255 million extension contract with the Eagles, making him the highest-paid player in NFL history.

Assembling an all-female management team was a deliberate choice for Hurts, a testament to his belief in equality and his desire to challenge gender stereotypes in the sports industry. Alongside Nicole Lynn, Hurts works with a team of talented women who bring their expertise and experience from various areas of sports management.

Chantal Romain (Media Relations and Client Services) brings a wealth of experience in communications strategies to Jalen Hurts' team. With a background that includes working with prestigious sports associations such as the NBA, WNBA, NBA G League, and the NFL, Romain's expertise in building and maintaining relationships with the press ensures that Hurts' story is effectively communicated to the public, maximizing his visibility and impact.

Shakeemah Simmons-Winter (Media Relations and Client Services) has prior experience as a senior publicist for the FIBA and the NFL and as the PR coordinator for the New York Knicks. Her ability to craft compelling narratives and manage media engagements is instrumental in shaping Hurts' public image and expanding his reach beyond the football field.

Managing the day-to-day operations and logistics of an NFL player's career requires exceptional organizational skills and attention to detail. **Jenna Malphrus** is responsible for overseeing Jalen Hurts' management tasks. From coordinating schedules and travel arrangements to handling contract logistics, Malphrus ensures that Hurts can focus on what he does best: playing football. Her dedication and efficiency make her an invaluable member of the team.

Marketing is crucial in establishing a player's brand and maximizing their earning potential. **Rachel Everett** is the mastermind behind Jalen Hurts' marketing efforts. Everett has spent over 13 years at the forefront of sports marketing, establishing a lasting legacy based on unwavering dedication and unparalleled expertise in athlete representation and activation.

As one of the driving forces and co-founders of ESM Sports, Everett is a true pioneer, seamlessly combining innovation, strategic thinking, and a deep understanding of the sports industry.

Renowned athletes such as Jalen Hurts, Nick Chubb, and D'Andre Swift are at the core of Rachel's impressive portfolio. Through her skillful storytelling and establishment of strategic partnerships, she has elevated their profiles and secured lucrative endorsement deals. In 2024, she added NFL rookie Jordan Travis, an alumnus of her alma mater, FSU, to her roster. In professional golf, Rachel guides LPGA standout Ally Ewing's off-field endeavors.

What sets Rachel apart is her unique approach, which involves integrating philanthropy into her partnerships. From supporting Boys and Girls Clubs to enhancing educational environments in Philadelphia schools, she goes beyond leveraging athletes' influence and Name, Image, and Likeness (NIL) for financial gain. Instead, she emphasizes the importance of positively impacting society as a whole.

But Rachel's contributions don't stop there. In 2023, she spearheaded the inaugural SupHER Bowl, a groundbreaking initiative to showcase, support, and inspire women in sports and beyond. With the backing of Champs Sports and Stanley, this exclusive event treated 40 influential women in sports to a lavish mansion experience in Arizona during Super Bowl Week. The SupHER Bowl provides a unique platform for women in sports. It enables brands to turn their commitment to equality into tangible actions, fostering equal opportunities on and off the court. Rachel Everett continues to reshape the sports narrative, advocating for inclusivity and creating pathways for athletes to shine.

The story of Jalen Hurts' all-female management team is about much more than football and contracts. It is a story of breaking barriers, challenging norms, and inspiring future generations. By assembling a team of talented women from diverse backgrounds, Hurts sends a powerful message that gender should never limit one's ability to succeed in any field.

♥

CHAPTER NINE:
NON-BINARY AND THIRD GENDER RECOGNITION AND THE LAW

In many countries around the world, individuals whose gender identities do not conform to the traditional male/female binary have been fighting for years to obtain official documents that reflect their true identities. The struggle for non-binary and third-gender recognition is more than just a bureaucratic battle; it is a human rights issue that has far-reaching implications for individuals' private lives and social acceptance.

Gender variant individuals have existed throughout history and across cultures. Some societies have recognized and celebrated gender identities beyond the binary, such as hijra communities in South Asia, two-spirit people among Native American cultures, the Waria in Southeast Asia, and Fa'afafine in Pacific Islander communities. However, the imposition of colonial rule introduced bureaucratic systems of gender assignment that forced individuals into binary classifications. Despite this, these communities persist and continue to provide alternative ways of thinking about gender that challenge traditional norms.

The European Court of Human Rights recognized the conflict between social reality and the law in a landmark 2002 decision. While the case addressed the transition between female and male genders, the court's ruling emphasized the serious interference with private life that occurs when the government fails to recognize an individual's gender identity.

This interference is particularly pronounced for those who do not identify as either female or male. The court's ruling indicates that compelling individuals to choose between traditional gender markers is a form of interference that should be mitigated.

The trans rights movement has long championed the idea that an individual's gender is determined by what they feel in their hearts and minds, not by their physical characteristics. This belief is encapsulated in the axiom, "Your sex is what's between your legs; your gender is what's between your ears." Just as transgender activists have fought for the right to change their official sex markers, non-binary activists question why anyone should be forced to choose between the limited options of female or male when there are countless variations of gender identities.

While progress has been made in recognizing non-binary gender identities, the journey towards full acceptance and legal recognition is far from over. At least ten countries currently allow individuals to choose an "X" gender marker under certain circumstances, although progress has often been slow and required lengthy court battles. In some cases, courts have only granted "X" gender markers to intersex individuals who are born with sex characteristics that do not fit typical definitions of male or female. This approach is rooted in outdated notions that gender markers should be based on biology or physical attributes.

LEGAL CHALLENGES AND HUMAN RIGHTS ADVOCACY

Gender-diverse and nonbinary individuals often find themselves caught in a spiral of exclusion and marginalization. They may face bullying at school, rejection from family members, homelessness, and limited employment opportunities. These challenges are amplified for individuals who belong to ethnic minorities, are migrants, live with HIV, or engage in sex work. This intersectionality exposes them to a higher risk of violence, including physical assault, rape, and other forms of abuse.

The struggle for recognition is further exacerbated by the lack of legal gender recognition in many countries. When their official documents do not reflect their gender identity, trans individuals face additional barriers and discrimination. They may encounter difficulties accessing healthcare, housing, social security, and freedom of movement. These challenges perpetuate stigma and prejudice, denying them basic human rights.

In the United Kingdom, the Court of Appeal ruled in March 2020 that human rights norms did not impose a positive obligation on the state to provide an "X" marker option in passports. This ruling came as a disappointment to non-binary activist Christie Elan-Cane, who had brought the case to secure a non-binary gender marker on their passport. Elan-Cane described the impact of the ruling as being told to continue to "collude in their own social invisibility." This decision highlights the ongoing challenges faced by non-binary individuals in achieving legal recognition of their gender identities.

Recognition of non-binary and third gender identities is not just a matter of bureaucratic convenience; it is about upholding the rights and dignity of individuals who do not fit into traditional gender categories. A 2018 survey conducted by the UK Government Equalities Office found that 7% of respondents identified as non-binary, with 52% of transgender respondents identifying as non-binary. Many participants in the survey expressed the harm they experienced when forced to choose a binary gender on official forms. By recognizing the identity of those who do not identify as female or male, governments can demonstrate their commitment to respecting the rights and dignity of all citizens.

The recognition of non-binary and third gender identities varies from country to country. Some nations have implemented progressive laws and policies enabling individuals to change their gender identity on official documents. Argentina, for example, passed the Gender Identity Law in 2012, allowing transgender individuals to change their gender markers without undergoing medical procedures or counseling. In Australia, individuals can choose an "X" gender marker on their passports and other official documents. Belgium's Constitutional Court has recently struck down parts of the country's transgender law, calling for the inclusion of a third gender option.

Evolving interpretations of human rights law suggest that third gender recognition is gaining momentum. Regional courts in Latin America and Europe have already affirmed that countries must allow citizens to change their gender markers from female to male or vice versa. It seems only a matter of time before a similar norm is established around the right to a gender identity that is neither male nor female, or encompasses both. Even global bureaucratic entities like the International Civil Aviation Organization (ICAO) have recognized the need for a third gender category, allowing for the designation of "X" in machine-readable passports.

DEPATHOLOGIZING TRANS IDENTITIES

For years, mental health diagnoses have been misused to pathologize gender identities. However, there has been a positive shift towards depathologizing trans identities. In 2019, the World Health Assembly revised the International Classification of Diseases (ICD-11), removing trans-related categories from the chapter on mental and behavioral disorders. This important step forward acknowledges that being transgender is not a mental illness and helps combat stigma and discrimination against trans individuals.

While the depathologization of trans identities is a significant milestone, it is essential to recognize that it will take time to
eradicate the deep-rooted societal perceptions that contribute to
the stigmatization of gender diversity. States are encouraged to
review their medical classifications based on the ICD-11, adopt
proactive measures to eliminate social stigma, and provide accessible and inclusive healthcare services to trans individuals.

THE FALLOUT OF INEQUITY IN THE UNITED STATES

Over the past few decades, the LGBTQ+ community in the
United States has taken significant strides towards achieving
equal rights and protections. However, despite these advancements, there has been a disturbing trend of anti-LGBTQ+ laws
being proposed and passed at the state level. These laws not
only threaten the hard-won progress but also have far-reaching consequences on the health and well-being of LGBTQ+
individuals. Just some of the potential negative fallout includes:

Social stress

Anti-LGBTQ+ laws create a hostile environment that exac-
erbates the stress and mental health disparities faced by
LGBTQ+ individuals. These laws send a message of exclusion and contribute to the marginalization and stigmatization
of the LGBTQ+ community. The fear of discrimination and
the need to hide one's identity can lead to increased rates of
depression, anxiety, and suicidality among LGBTQ+ individuals.

Silencing discussions about sexual orientation and gender identity in public school classrooms, as seen in laws like
Florida's HB 1557, further perpetuates feelings of shame and

isolation. These stressors can have detrimental effects on both the mental and physical health of LGBTQ+ individuals, potentially leading to increased rates of cardiovascular disease, hypertension, and unhealthy coping behaviors like smoking and substance use.

Decreased social support and increased violence

Anti-LGBTQ+ laws not only impact individuals but also have significant interpersonal consequences. The silencing of discussions about LGBTQ+ identities in schools can erode potential sources of social support for LGBTQ+ youth. Teachers and staff may feel restricted in their ability to provide support, leading to increased bullying and teasing among students. LGBTQ+ youth may also feel pressured to hide their identities and avoid discussions about their families, further isolating them from their peers. The lack of social support in schools can have long-term impacts on mental health and may contribute to unhealthy relationships in adulthood.

Moreover, anti-LGBTQ+ laws can fuel hate crimes and violence against LGBTQ+ individuals. When laws send a message of exclusion, they embolden individuals with homophobic or transphobic beliefs, leading to an increased risk of violence. The fear of violence and discrimination can deter LGBTQ+ individuals from reporting crimes to authorities, further perpetuating a cycle of marginalization and lack of legal protection. Marginalized groups are seen as "less worthy" or "less important," and therefore, they do not warrant the benefit of our society's morals – we think of the group's members as fair game for physical, emotional and financial abuses, or we simply don't think of them at all and completely fail to recognize their needs as a group.

Implications for policies and practices

Anti-LGBTQ+ laws not only affect individuals and interpersonal relationships but also have broader policy and practice implications. These laws undermine efforts to achieve health equity for LGBTQ+ individuals and perpetuate systemic discrimination. They create barriers to accessing healthcare, education, and employment opportunities, limiting the overall well-being and quality of life for LGBTQ+ individuals. It is essential to recognize the political determinants of health and address the power dynamics at play in policymaking to dismantle discriminatory practices and promote equality.

UNDERSTANDING POWER AND INTERSECTIONALITY

To effectively address the impacts of anti-LGBTQ+ laws, it is crucial to adopt theoretical approaches that emphasize power dynamics and intersectionality.

Power plays a significant role in shaping outcomes, and an understanding of power structures is vital in dismantling discriminatory practices. But what does this mean, exactly? Power structures are the high-level systems that have been "in charge" of how things run for so long that many of us take them for granted. These can be specific groups, like government bodies or company boards of directors, or more nebulous organizational beliefs like the US public school system or simply "the way things have always been."

Power structures promote systemic inequities, both intentionally and unintentionally. Intentional inequity quite boldly says, "We don't recognize these people as equal," and though it is shocking, it's at least easy to spot and outlaw. The unintentional variety is systemic bias, rooted in longstanding beliefs and practices, which is a far greater challenge to conquer. For example, the idea that there are only two genders is a long-standing belief that many people find difficult to overcome.

Therefore, when we say that understanding power, and power structures, is vital to address the impact of LGBTQ+ legislation, we're actually referring to a couple of dynamics. First, laws have to be made on a power-structure level. Second, we must address not just overt inequity but covert inequity by looking for systemic bias in these systems.

Intersectionality recognizes that individuals have multiple social identities that intersect and interact with one another, influencing their experiences of discrimination and oppression. By employing these theoretical frameworks, researchers and advocates can better understand the complex interplay between social identities and work towards inclusive policies and practices.

Methodological approaches that prioritize collaborative engagement between researchers and community members are essential in understanding the impacts of anti-LGBTQ+ laws. Researchers must work directly with LGBTQ+ communities to ensure that their perspectives and experiences are accurately represented in the research. Additionally, disrupting power imbalances is crucial in conducting research that challenges discriminatory practices. By giving voice to marginalized communities and centering their experiences, researchers can contribute to a more comprehensive understanding of the impacts of anti-LGBTQ+ laws.

Public health researchers play an essential role in reversing harmful policies that negatively affect LGBTQ+ individuals and undermine health equity. Research should focus on understanding the individual, interpersonal, and systemic consequences of anti-LGBTQ+ laws. By highlighting the detrimental impacts of these laws, researchers can provide evidence-based arguments for policy change and advocate for the rights and well-being of LGBTQ+ individuals. It is crucial to adopt an approach that is attentive to power differences and disrupts existing power imbalances to promote health equity and inclusivity for all.

WHAT CITIZENS CAN DO: ADVOCACY AND ACTIVISM

Advocacy and activism are powerful ways to support nonbinary and transgender rights. Here are some steps you can take:

Stay informed. Stay up to date on current issues, policies, and legislation affecting nonbinary and transgender individuals. Follow reputable organizations and activists working towards equality.

Contact elected officials. Reach out to your elected officials and express your support for nonbinary and transgender rights. Advocate for inclusive policies, healthcare access, and legal protections. If you don't know where to begin, look to the LGBTQI+ Working Group of the Civil Rights Division of the US Department of Justice, at https://www.justice.gov/crt/lgbtqi-working-group. This is an excellent resource where you can find the current status of legal and policy issues about discrimination based on "sexual orientation, gender identity, intersex status, and HIV/AIDS status."

Participate in campaigns. Join or support campaigns and initiatives that promote nonbinary and transgender rights. Attend rallies, sign petitions, and use social media to raise awareness and promote change. However, if attending events or socializing isn't your cup of tea, you can also...

Support LGBTQ+ organizations. Donate to and volunteer with LGBTQ+ organizations that provide resources, support, and advocacy for non-binary and transgender individuals. In the upcoming chapter on becoming an ally to the LGBTQ+ community, I will share a list of organizations supporting protection and services for the community that need money, time and volunteers.

LEGAL GENDER RECOGNITION: A DISTANT DREAM?

Legal gender recognition is a fundamental aspect of an individual's identity. It encompasses the right to be recognized and treated according to one's self-determined gender. Unfortunately, many trans individuals face significant obstacles in obtaining legal recognition of their gender identity. Some countries impose burdensome requirements, such as medical certification, surgery, sterilization, or divorce, which can be invasive, costly, and unnecessary.

The lack of access to legal gender recognition not only denies trans individuals their rights but also perpetuates discrimination, exclusion, and violence in various aspects of life. It limits their access to healthcare, housing, social security, and employment opportunities. To ensure full equality and inclusion, states must adopt legislation and policies that facilitate a simple, accessible, and non-discriminatory process for gender recognition. This proccss should be based on self-determination, not require invasive medical or legal requirements, and recognize non-binary identities.

Legislation plays a significant role in protecting the rights of gender-diverse individuals. Anti-discrimination laws should explicitly include gender identity as a protected ground, and hate crimes legislation should recognize transphobia as an aggravating factor for sentencing. Collecting data on violence and discrimination against trans and gender-diverse individuals is crucial for informing policies, addressing gaps in investigations and prosecution, and providing effective remedies.

States should also take affirmative action to redress structural discrimination and socioeconomic inequalities. By implementing these measures and fostering a culture of acceptance and respect, we can create a society that embraces gender diversity and promotes the well-being and rights of all individuals.

Anti-LGBTQ+ laws have far-reaching consequences on the health and well-being of LGBTQ+ individuals. These laws perpetuate stigma, marginalization, and discrimination, leading to increased rates of mental health disparities, violence, and diminished social support. To effectively address the impacts of these laws, theoretical approaches that emphasize power dynamics and intersectionality should guide research efforts.

Collaborative engagement between researchers and community members is crucial, as is disrupting power imbalances to ensure that marginalized voices are heard. Public health researchers have a responsibility to advocate for policy change and work towards dismantling discriminatory practices. By promoting health equity and inclusivity, we can create a society that values and respects the rights of all individuals, regardless of their sexual orientation or gender identity.

♥

CHAPTER TEN:
KNOW THE LGBTQ+ MOVEMENT

As I have researched and considered how best to discuss becoming an active ally or even a sponsor of the LGBTQ community, common threads have emerged. Consistently, the research says one thing we can all do to improve our allyship is to understand the history of the movement. The LGBTQ+ community's history in the United States didn't just begin a couple of decades ago when someone made a flag! The gay community has always been present, just frequently hidden from sight.

Understanding the history of LGBTQ+ activism is vital to becoming an informed ally. When we recognize key events, milestones, and leaders in the LGBTQ+ rights movement, and understand the struggles and achievements of the past, we can better support ongoing efforts for equality.

This chapter delves into the rich history of the LGBTQ+ rights movement in the United States. It highlights significant events, key figures, and the progress made towards equality and acceptance.

From the establishment of the United States itself, the abolishing of slavery, the recognition of women as equal citizens, the formation of the first gay rights organizations, the election of LGBTQ+ politicians, and landmark court rulings, this timeline showcases the resilience and determination of the LGBTQ+ community. I include several events marking progress for other equality issues, because any such progress is a notable moment for marginalized groups. Seeing how the timeline of these various human rights movements coincide is fascinating.

Remember, however, that this list pertains mostly to the United States and is by no means comprehensive! In a massive group encompassing activists, artists, athletes, and politicians, countless prominent figures made significant contributions to the LGBTQ+ movement. Their resilience, advocacy, and determination have paved the way for progress and continue to inspire generations. There have been countless contributors and important moments to the movement, each one a story unto itself. I hope this list inspires you to learn even more.

LGBTQ+ TIMELINE

1607: The founding of Jamestown, Virginia, marked the establishment of the first permanent English settlement in America.

1619: Slavery was introduced to the United States when approximately 20 Africans were sold into slavery in Jamestown, Virginia, marking the beginning of a dark era of racial inequality.

1620: The establishment of colonial Plymouth brought forth Puritan norms that emphasized the nuclear family unit and strict gender roles.

1624: Richard Cornish of the Virginia Colony was tried and hanged for sodomy, highlighting the persecution faced by LGBTQ+ individuals during this time.

1630: The Massachusetts Bay Colony was established, with the aim of creating an ideal Christian community based on Puritan religious and moral beliefs.

1649: Sarah White Norman and Mary Vincent Hammon were charged with "lewd behavior" in Plymouth, Massachusetts. The pair is believed to be the first convicted for lesbian behavior in the New World.

1691: Virginia passed the first anti-miscegenation law in

1691, forbidding interracial marriage, further perpetuating discrimination and inequality.

1714: Sodomy laws were in place in the early colonies and the colonial militia, contributing to the persecution and marginalization of LGBTQ+ individuals.

1775: The population of enslaved individuals in the colonies reached nearly 500,000, highlighting the systemic oppression faced by marginalized communities. Then, just a year later...

1776: The signing of the Declaration of Independence in 1776 marked a pivotal moment in American history, emphasizing the ideals of liberty and equality.

1778: Lieutenant Gotthold Frederick Enslin became the first documented service member dismissed from the US military for homosexuality, highlighting early discrimination faced by LGBTQ+ individuals.

1779: Thomas Jefferson proposed a law in Virginia to make sodomy punishable by mutilation, reflecting the prevailing negative attitudes towards homosexuality at the time.

1788: The adoption of the US Constitution, which included the three-fifths clause, reinforced racial inequality and discrimination against enslaved individuals. The infamous three-fifth's clause stated in Article One, Section Two that "any person who is not free would be counted as three-fifths of a free individual for the purposes of determining congressional representation." The clause gave much more power to slave-holding states. (The clause was repealed by the Reconstruction Amendments that followed the Civil War.)

1789: Olaudah Equiano, a formerly enslaved person, published *The Interesting Narrative of the Life of Olaudah Equiano*, which shed light on same-sex relationships within the slave community.

1839: Women's rights activist Margaret Fuller hosted conversations about gender roles and women's rights, challenging societal norms and advocating for increased autonomy for women.

1845: Margaret Fuller published "The Great Lawsuit," urging women to assert their independence and challenge the traditional role assigned to them.

1848: The Seneca Falls Convention marked the first women's rights convention, paving the way for the fight for gender equality. Meanwhile, the discovery of gold in California led to a massive influx of people, predominantly men, creating a unique social environment. For example...

1849: Jason Chamberlain and John Chaffee, a same-sex couple, embarked on a journey to seek their fortunes in the California gold rush, highlighting the diversity of relationships during this time.[8]

Also during this year, Elizabeth Blackwell became the first woman to graduate medical school and become a doctor in the United States.

1851: Former enslaved person Sojourner Truth delivered her famous "Ain't I a Woman?" speech at the Women's Rights Convention in Akron, Ohio.

1852: J.D. Bothwick reported attending a "miners' ball," an event exclusive to men, in Angels Camp, California, offering a glimpse into the social dynamics of the gold rush era.

1857-1861: President James Buchanan, believed by some historians to be gay, had a longterm relationship with William Rufus King, the Vice President under Franklin Pierce.

1861: Sarah Emma Edmonds and Jennie Hodgers disguised themselves as men and fought in the Union army during the Civil War, challenging gender norms and expectations.

1868: The ratification of the Fourteenth Amendment, which guarantees equal protection under the law, becomes

---

8 I found it quite interesting that the migration of men to California formed a populated sector with an almost exclusively male population. When I relayed this information to a friend, he looked thoughtful and then said, "Hmm, maybe the Gold Rush wasn't all about the gold."

a cornerstone for future civil rights cases, including those related to LGBTQ+ rights.

1868: We'wha, a Zuni Native American who identified as Two-Spirit, met with President Grover Cleveland, showcasing the rich diversity of gender identities and expressions.

1869: Hungarian journalist Karl-Maria Kertbeny coined the term "homosexual," contributing to the understanding and recognition of same-sex attraction.

Wyoming became the first state to grant women the right to vote and hold office.

Susan B. Anthony and Elizabeth Cady Stanton founded the National Woman Suffrage Association.

1879: Charley Parkhurst, a stagecoach driver in Central California, lived as a man despite being assigned female at birth, highlighting early transgender experiences.

1886: Henry James's book, *The Bostonians*, shed light on "Boston Marriages," long-term relationships between two women that defied societal norms.

1889: Jane Addams and other women established Hull House in Chicago, providing support and resources for women and challenging traditional gender roles.

1890: The term "bisexual" was included in a medical dictionary, further contributing to the understanding and recognition of bisexuality as a valid sexual orientation. In 1894, The term "bisexual" was mentioned in the translated version of the pamphlet *Psychopathia Sexualis*.

1892: The term "lesbian" was included in a medical dictionary, recognizing same-sex attraction between women.

1896: The Supreme Court's decision in Plessy v. Ferguson upheld racial segregation, perpetuating discrimination and racial inequality.

1901: Henry Gerber founded the Society for Human Rights in Chicago, the United States' first documented gay rights organization.

1917 (approximately): Born Alberta Lucille Hart in 1890,

Dr. Alan Hart had a hysterectomy, making him one of the first trans men in the United States to undergo surgery. Dr. Hart was a pioneer in radiology and tuberculosis study and wrote several books promoting social change.

1920: Ratification of the 19th Amendment gives women the right to vote.

1924: The Society for Human Rights published the first recorded gay rights newsletter, *Friendship and Freedom*, establishing a platform for LGBTQ+ advocacy.

1950: The early national gay rights organization, the Mattachine Society, was founded. Though it was not the first gay rights organization, the Mattachine Society is one of the more famous due to its founder, Harry Hay and his ties to communism. Hay originally began the group as a way for "bachelors" to become more socially active and unified, participating in protests, fundraising and education. The influence of the group was quite widespread.

1955: *One: The Homosexual Magazine* challenged censorship and discrimination, leading to a landmark Supreme Court ruling in favor of homosexuals' First Amendment rights. In the case *One, Inc. v. Oleson* US 371, the court ruled that pro-homosexual writing is not obscene per se. While the term "gay" had been used in Europe earlier, 1955 marked the year when it became widely associated with same-sex relationships between men.

This year, Rosa Parks refused to give up her seat on the bus in Montgomery, Alabama, one of the events that inspired the launch of the civil rights movement.

1963: Bayard Rustin played a crucial role in shaping the movement for equality. Rustin's commitment to nonviolent protest and his organizational skills made him a trusted advisor to Martin Luther King Jr. He was instrumental in organizing the historic March on Washington in 1963, where King delivered the unforgettable "I Have a Dream" speech. Despite his invaluable contributions, Rustin faced discrimination and prejudice within the movement due to his sexual orientation. As an openly gay man, Rustin experienced societal backlash and even legal repercussions. However, his unwavering dedication to justice and equality persisted, and his influence continues.

1965: John Oliven's book, *Sexual Hygiene and Pathology*, introduced the term "transgender," acknowledging individuals who identify with a gender different from their assigned sex at birth.

This was also the year in which the black LGBTQ+ population of Philadelphia organized a picket line and sit-in at Dewey's Coffee Shop for its refusal to serve young people in "non-conformist clothing." The restaurant agreed to end its discriminatory policies.

1967: The Sexual Freedom League was formed in San Francisco to support bisexual individuals.

1969: This was the year of *the* landmark event in kicking off the LGBTQ+ movement. The Stonewall Inn raid and subsequent riots surrounding Christopher Park in Greenwich Village, New York City, ignited the modern LGBTQ+ rights movement, empowering activists and paving the way for future progress.

Also known as the Stonewall uprising or the Stonewall rebellion, this action began after police raided the Stonewall Inn on the morning of June 28, 1968. Until this time, raids on gay bars (which were illegal) were commonplace in the United States. But the cultural revolution, including the civil rights movement, sparked the gay community to react to oppression. Though the Stonewall Inn had been raided numerous times before, that early morning's raid did not proceed as usual. Customers refused to produce identification or submit to searches as usual, prompting police frustration.

Those patrons who were allowed to leave, who would normally have scattered, instead remained outside the bar, drawing a crowd. Soon a large group gathered outside, most of whom were gay, and they began to mock and boo the police who tried to escort arrestees outside. When a woman was beaten by the police in front of the crowd, she shouted to them for help and the mob became incensed, overturning police vehicles; the police responded with violence against several members of the crowd. Soon the Stonewall Inn was in flames. The riots escalated for several days after that as greater numbers of gay liberation groups and organizations joined.

In the aftermath of Stonewall, notable figures in the gay rights movement emerged. **Miss Major Griffin-Gracy** dedicated her life to advocating for the rights and well-being of transgender and gender nonconforming individuals. As a veteran of the Stonewall uprising in 1969, she witnessed firsthand the power of collective action and community resilience. After her release from prison, Miss Major became an influential figure in supporting transgender individuals who were incarcerated. She co-founded the Transgender Gender Variant Intersex Justice Project, an organization that advocates for the rights of transgender people within the criminal justice system.

Through her tireless work, Miss Major has uplifted the voices of marginalized communities, fought against systemic discrimination, and provided much-needed support to those in need. Her advocacy continues to inspire and empower transgender individuals around the world.

Trailblazing drag king **Storme DeLarverie** played a pivotal role in the LGBTQ+ community's fight for equality. Frequently called the Rosa Parks of the gay community, DeLarverie was also a key figure during the Stonewall uprising in 1969.

As a biracial lesbian, DeLarverie experienced discrimination and prejudice throughout her life. Her performances as a drag king challenged societal norms and provided a platform for self-expression and liberation. DeLarverie's courage and resilience continue to inspire individuals to embrace their true identities and defy societal expectations.

1970: On June 28, Christopher Street Liberation Day held an assembly on the street outside the Stonewall Inn, marking the first anniversary of the Stonewall Riots; at the same time, parades were held in Los Angeles and Chicago. These were **the first Gay Pride marches in US History**. Each subsequent year, marches spread to major towns across the United States and worldwide.

Also in 1970, James McConnell and Richard Baker of Minneapolis applied for the first gay marriage license. The license was denied by the Clerk of the District Court.

1974: The American Psychiatric Association removed homosexuality from its list of mental illnesses, challenging widespread discrimination and stigmatization.

1977: Transgender tennis player Renee Richards won her lawsuit before the Supreme Court of New York to compete in the female category of the US Open.

1978: Harvey Milk, the first non-incumbent, openly gay male elected to office in the State of California, was assassinated. The following year, his shooter, Dan White, received what was perceived as overly lenient sentencing when he was only convicted of voluntary manslaughter, sparking the White Night riots.

1980s: Playwright Larry Kramer emerged as a prominent figure in the fight against the AIDS epidemic. Frustrated by the government's inadequate response, Kramer co-founded the AIDS Coalition to Unleash Power (ACT UP), an organization that demanded increased funding for research, improved healthcare, and an end to discrimination against people living with HIV/AIDS. Kramer's impassioned speeches and writings brought attention to the urgency of the crisis and pushed for change. He was unapologetically vocal in his criticism of government officials, pharmaceutical companies, and the medical establishment. Kramer's activism helped mobilize the LGBTQ+ community and allies, leading to significant advancements in AIDS research, treatment, and public awareness.

1983: Congressperson Gerry Studds came out, becoming the first openly gay member of Congress.

1996: The Stonewall Inn, Christopher Park, and surrounding areas were designated as the Stonewall National Monument, recognizing their historical significance in advancing LGBTQ+ rights.

2011: "Don't Ask, Don't Tell" was formally repealed. The process to repeal began in 2010, to end the policy that declared gay men and women from openly serving in the military. "Don't Ask, Don't Tell" had been policy since 1994, when it was instituted by the Clinton Administration. While in retrospect, the policy is discriminatory and troubling, in 1994 it was actually viewed by many as a step forward, purportedly allowing gays to freely serve in the military, provided they were discreet about their sexual orientation.

2012: Wisconsin's Tammy Baldwin is the first openly gay politician elected to the US Senate.

The Black Lives Matter movement erupted from the murder of 17-year-old Trayvon Martin in February of that year.

2015: The Supreme Court's ruling in Obergefell v. Hodges legalized same-sex marriage nationwide, a landmark victory for the LGBTQ+ community and a major step towards equality.

2016: New York issued the United States' first intersex birth certificate.

2017: The first openly transgender candidate is elected to a state legislature, as Virginia's House of Delegates elected Danica Roem.

2018: U.S. Representative Jarid Polis is elected governor of Colorado and becomes the nation's first openly gay state governor.

TWO STEPS BACK: TRUMP'S RECORD OF ACTION AGAINST TRANSGENDER PEOPLE

The LGBTQ+ rights movement in America has been marked by significant milestones, from the establishment of the first gay rights organizations to the legalization of same-sex marriage. Despite facing discrimination and adversity, the LGBTQ+ community has shown resilience and determination in the fight for equality and acceptance. As we continue to progress, it is crucial to recognize the contributions of activists and allies who have paved the way for a more inclusive and compassionate society.

However, discrimination against the LGBTQ+ community remains extremely problematic; its members are frequently exposed to biases, hatred and crime, up to and including murder. In the past decade, prejudice was made significantly worse. A wave of extreme conservativism has brought an intense backlash against the community, particularly against nonbinary and transgender individuals; it has become alarmingly socially "acceptable" to express hatred toward marginalized groups, and the LGBTQ+ community is a prime target.

From his inauguration, President Trump's administration launched a relentless assault on the rights of LGBTQ people, specifically targeting transgender individuals. These policies have had far-reaching consequences, perpetuating discrimination and marginalization. Let's examine some of the major changes implemented or attempted by the Trump administration:

Rollback of protections in housing and homeless services. In July 2020, the Department of Housing and Urban Development announced the rollback of a previous rule that protected transgender people from discrimination in homeless shelters and other housing services receiving federal funds. This action left vulnerable transgender individuals at an increased risk of homelessness and further marginalization.

Undermining healthcare protections. In June 2020, the Department of Health and Human Services finalized a rule that rolled back protections against healthcare discrimination for transgender individuals. This rule allowed healthcare providers to deny necessary care or insurance coverage based on gender identity, leaving many transgender individuals without access to vital healthcare services.

Attacks on transgender students' rights. The Department of Education issued a letter in May 2020, declaring that the federal Title IX rule required schools to ban transgender students from participating in school sports. This discriminatory policy not only infringed upon the rights of transgender students but also perpetuated harmful stereotypes and exclusion.

Elimination of data collection on sexual orientation and gender identity. The Department of Health and Human Services published a final rule in May 2020, eliminating the collection of sexual orientation and gender identity data on foster youth and foster and adoptive parents. This erasure of data further hindered efforts to address the specific needs and challenges faced by transgender individuals within the foster care system.

Threats to transgender students' access to education. The Department of Education's final rule, published in May 2020, also weakened protections for transgender students by allowing schools to exclude transgender students from facilities and activities that aligned with their gender identity. This policy created an unsafe and hostile environment for transgender students, denying them equal access to education.

CONCLUSION

The past decade has brought the rights and experiences of transgender and nonbinary individuals to the forefront of public discourse. We have seen both progress and setbacks in the fight for transgender and nonbinary rights. Government policies and legal decisions have had a profound impact on the lives of transgender individuals, either perpetuating discrimination or promoting inclusivity, and often perpetuating prejudice and discrimination against this marginalized community.

Looking at the timeline of progress for LGBTQ+ rights, and seeing how quickly this progress can be injured, perhaps undone, by thoughtless, biased policies is heartbreaking. The LGBTQ+ community is strong and resolved, but it needs support from the outside as well. No one needs to stand by helplessly and let these hateful things happen. In the next two chapters, we will discuss allyship, looking at ways that we can promote equity in our homes, workplaces and communities. By understanding the struggles faced by transgender and non-binary individuals, we can work towards dismantling prejudice, advocating for policy changes, and creating a society that embraces and respects gender diversity.

CHAPTER ELEVEN:
BEING AN ALLY

Being an ally to the LGBTQ+ community is about more than just saying you support equal human rights. It's about advocating for and empowering marginalized individuals, challenging oppression, and creating a safe and inclusive environment for all. That's incredibly important.

But as I discovered when I wrote *Bridging the Gap*, there are varying levels of support, and real sponsorship of any marginalized groups means more than just a friendliness and acceptance – it means opening doors for them, inviting them to the table, and supporting them in an open and public way.

This behavior is not without risks; supporting a highly controversial group may put us in a similar line of danger (shunning, mockery, even violence) that group faces regularly. That's why such support conveys our message loud and clear: we are willing to take a risk to show solidarity. If you're ready to take your allyship to the next level, I'll provide you with the knowledge and tools to be an awesome and active LGBTQ+ ally – and, in broad strokes, an ally to any marginalized group you wish to support and sponsor.

As we move forward, please know that I applaud allyship in all its forms. You need not take up a flag and march to be an ally. Being an ally begins with simple manners: acceptance and respect toward people no matter who they are. If we could convince the entire world to accept and respect everyone equally, there would be little need for activism! So never think that I discount the day-to-day interactions that promote equity in our homes, workplaces and communities. We'll begin with the simple things.

WHAT ISSUES DOES THE LGBTQ+ COMMUNITY FACE?

To be good allies, we must understand the prejudices and difficulties faced by our LGBTQ+ friends. Currently, the major issues facing the community nationwide include:

Achieving gender identity recognition. Transgender individuals often face legal challenges when their gender identity does not align with the sex assigned at birth. Many countries lack comprehensive gender recognition laws, leaving transgender individuals without legal recognition and perpetuating stigma and prejudice against them. In effect, this means that in many cultures, if one is not cisgender, one does not qualify as a human being in the eyes of the legal system. It sounds like science fiction, doesn't it?

The pathologization of transgender identities. Historically, mental health diagnoses have been misused to pathologize transgender identities, contributing to stigma and discrimination. However, there has been progress towards depathologizing transgender identities. Fortunately, the World Health Assembly adopted the eleventh revision of the International Classification of Diseases (ICD-11) in 2019, removing transgender-related categories from the chapter on mental and behavioral disorders. This revision is a significant step towards ensuring that transgender individuals can live free from violence and discrimination – on paper. One's job as an ally is ensuring that the LGBTQ+ community can live free from those stereotypes on a day-to-day basis.

Legal Gender Recognition and Access to Services. Access to legal gender recognition is crucial for transgender individuals to have their identities recognized and respected. However, many legal systems impose burdensome requirements, such as medical certification, surgery, or sterilization. The right to self-determination in legal gender recognition is a fundamental aspect of individual identity.

Social Inclusion and Ending Violence. To foster social inclusion and combat violence against transgender individuals, comprehensive measures are necessary. Sensitization campaigns, education policies, and media portrayals that challenge stereotypes and misconceptions are crucial for creating a more inclusive society. Additionally, collecting data on violence and discrimination against transgender individuals is essential for informing policies and addressing gaps in investigations and remedies.

Serving Trans and Nonbinary Survivors of Domestic and Sexual Violence. Transgender and nonbinary individuals face alarmingly high rates of domestic and sexual violence. The 2015 US Transgender Survey revealed staggering statistics, with nearly half of respondents experiencing verbal harassment, and nearly one in ten experiencing physical attacks due to their transgender identity. Moreover, the survey highlighted that communities of color and those with intersecting identities face even higher rates of violence.

Now, we will discuss how allies can support these global causes on a local level.

WHAT DOES IT MEAN TO BE AN "ALLY"?

An ally is someone who stands alongside marginalized communities, amplifying their voices and working towards social change. As an LGBTQ+ ally, your role is to support and advocate for LGBTQ+ individuals, challenge discrimination, and educate yourself and others about LGBTQ+ issues.

- Being an ally means taking intentional steps to educate yourself, engage in advocacy, and create inclusive spaces. It's about recognizing your privilege, learning from the LGBTQ+ community, and using your voice to make a positive impact.

- Being an ally means acknowledging and understanding the barriers that LGBTQ+ individuals still face today. Educate yourself about issues such as discrimination, healthcare disparities, and legal challenges. By being informed, you can effectively support and advocate for change.

- Being an ally is an ongoing journey of learning and growth. Embrace the fact that you may make mistakes along the way. When corrected, listen, reflect, and apologize. Learn from these experiences and commit to doing better in the future.

STEPS TOWARD ALLYSHIP

Becoming an ally means understanding a relatively new way of looking at gender identity. These are not "new" ways of being human, mind you, but ways of being human that have always existed and which we are now bringing out of hiding. To review, there are two important factors to remember:

1. **The difference between gender identity vs. biological sex**

   To support nonbinary and transgender individuals, it's essential to understand the difference between gender identity and biological sex. Gender identity refers to a person's internal sense of their own gender, which may or may not align with the sex they were assigned at birth. Biological sex, on the other hand, is determined by physical characteristics such as reproductive organs and chromosomes. Recognizing that gender identity is not solely determined by biological sex is a crucial step towards promoting inclusivity and acceptance.

2. **The meaning of nonbinary and transgender identities**

    Nonbinary individuals do not identify exclusively as male or female but exist outside of the traditional gender binary. They may experience their gender identity as a blend of both genders, fluid, or completely independent of the binary.

    Transgender individuals, on the other hand, have a gender identity that differs from the sex assigned to them at birth. It is important to respect the language and identities that individuals use to define themselves, as not all nonbinary individuals identify as transgender. Supporting and affirming their chosen identities is a cornerstone of promoting inclusivity.

Keeping these things in mind, here is how allyship begins, grows and prospers:

Challenge your biases

We all have biases, whether conscious or unconscious. It's essential to challenge and examine your own biases to create a more inclusive environment. Reflect on any preconceived notions or stereotypes you may hold about LGBTQ+ individuals and actively work to dismantle them.

Use the right words

Language plays a crucial role in creating an inclusive environment. Take the time to understand and use respectful terminology when discussing LGBTQ+ issues. Educate yourself on the meanings of terms such as gender identity, sexual orientation, and pronouns. Remember, the burden of education should not fall solely on LGBTQ+ individuals, so take the initiative to learn and grow.

I hope that the Identity Index in Chapter Two was a great start! And just a reminder: we discussed the use of pronouns in Chapter Three under the section titled "The basics, continuing with language."

Respect personal boundaries and identities

Respect individuals' pronouns, names, and identities. Use gender-neutral language when unsure, and apologize and correct yourself if you make a mistake. Creating a safe space means valuing and affirming everyone's authentic selves.

Practice active listening

Being an ally means being a good listener. Give space for LGBTQ+ individuals to share their experiences and perspectives. Be open to learning from their stories and avoid making assumptions. Actively listening fosters understanding and empathy. Have open and respectful conversations with non-binary and transgender individuals. Ask questions and learn from their experiences and perspectives.

Embrace intersectionality

Recognize that the LGBTQ+ experience is not the same for everyone. Intersectionality is the concept that people's identities and experiences are shaped by various intersecting factors, such as race, religion, disability, and gender. Embrace diverse perspectives and seek out voices from marginalized communities within the LGBTQ+ umbrella.

Be mindful of microaggressions

Microaggressions are subtle, everyday behaviors or comments that marginalize and invalidate individuals based on their identity. Be mindful of your language and actions to avoid unintentional microaggressions. Educate yourself about common microaggressions faced by LGBTQ+ individuals and actively work to eliminate them from your interactions.

Stand up and speak up

One of the most powerful ways to be an ally is to use your voice to speak out against discrimination. Stand up against homophobic, transphobic, or discriminatory remarks, even when LGBTQ+ individuals are not present. Support the person being targeted. By challenging harmful language and stereotypes, you create a safer and more inclusive environment for all. Your intervention can make a significant impact and send a clear message that discrimination will not be tolerated.

Be an advocate in your personal and professional life

As an ally, your impact extends beyond public activism. Advocate for LGBTQ+ inclusivity in your personal relationships, workplace, and community. Challenge policies and practices that discriminate against LGBTQ+ individuals and promote diversity and acceptance.

Regularly reflect on your allyship journey. Assess your actions, intentions, and impact. Seek feedback from LGBTQ+ individuals and be open to constructive criticism. By continuously evaluating your allyship, you can grow and improve as an advocate.

Celebrate diversity!

Promote and celebrate the diversity of the LGBTQ+ community. Attend Pride events, support LGBTQ+ artists and businesses, and engage with LGBTQ+ culture. By embracing diversity, you contribute to a more inclusive and vibrant society.

Use your platform for good

If you have a platform, whether it's on social media or within your community, use it to amplify LGBTQ+ voices and promote inclusivity. Share educational resources that promote visibility and understanding. Feature their personal stories, uplifting messages, artwork and achievements. By leveraging your influence, you can inspire and educate others.

PROMOTING INCLUSIVITY IN THE WORKPLACE

Creating an inclusive environment is essential for supporting nonbinary and transgender individuals. Here are some steps you can take to promote inclusivity:

- **Review policies and practices.** Ensure that workplace policies and practices are inclusive of nonbinary and transgender individuals. This includes using gender-inclusive language, providing gender-neutral restrooms, and implementing inclusive dress codes.

- **Educate staff and colleagues.** Offer training sessions and workshops to educate staff about gender diversity, inclusivity, and the importance of using correct pronouns.

- **Implement support measures.** Create support networks, employee resource groups, or counseling services specifically tailored to the needs of nonbinary and transgender individuals in the workplace.

- **Offer support and follow up.** Reach out to LGBTQ+ colleagues and offer your support. Let them know that you are there to listen, learn, and advocate for them. Regularly check in to see how they are doing and if there's anything you can do to support them. By demonstrating your care and concern, you create a sense of safety and belonging for LGBTQ+ employees.

- **Weed bias out of the systems.** Bias has a nasty tendency to slip into systems so discreetly that we fail to see what is staring at us right in the face. Review processes used for hiring, annual reviews, and promotions, and ensure that people are being judged on the quality of their work alone. In *Bridging the Gap*, I go into considerable detail about removing bias from systems to promote equity.

- **Foster visibility and representation.** Advocate for LGBTQ+ representation in leadership positions and decision-making roles within your organization. Encourage diverse voices to be heard and considered. Ensure LGBTQ+ employees have opportunities to contribute to projects, initiatives, and discussions that impact their work and the organization as a whole. By visibly celebrating LGBTQ+ diversity, you send a powerful message of acceptance and inclusion.

In **educational institutions**, further this support by:

- Establishing safe spaces within the institution where nonbinary and transgender students can seek support, connect with others, and find resources.

- Promoting gender-inclusive policies, such as allowing students to use their preferred names and pronouns, providing access to gender-neutral restrooms, and offering comprehensive LBGTQ+ education.

- Providing training for teachers, staff, and students to increase awareness and understanding of gender diversity, fostering a more inclusive learning environment.

SUPPORTING CHANGE AS IT HAPPENS

Mostly, the recommendations in this chapter apply universally to promoting equity and inclusiveness. However, there is one situation we should specifically address: when a person you know "comes out" – or basically tells you (and maybe others) that they are of a different gender or orientation than you had previously believed. This moment is important. The news may shock or surprise you, or it may not. It may dismay you, depending on the circumstances. It may fill you with joy that your friend or loved one is realizing more fully who they really are.

A guide for supporting your friend or loved one through change should be fairly self-explanatory. We do this all the time. We support people as they become spouses, parents, or divorcees, through career changes, grief, changes in personal beliefs, and illnesses. We manage to love people whose beliefs are different from ours. We manage to forgive people who hurt us. But a friend or loved one announcing, "I no longer identify as a woman or man," or "I am having gender-affirming surgery," is a slippery topic of support for the same reasons we have repeated often: the idea of more than two genders is new to us, and our society is experiencing dreadful growing pains when it comes to acceptance. So, I offer these tips:

Remember first and foremost: *it's not about you.* Your loved one's decision is *theirs*. It is not to hurt you, or to get even with you, or make you uncomfortable. Taking one of the most important decisions of their life and seeing it only from your personal viewpoint is not only unfair but also immature.

Honesty is a good policy here, provided the honesty is equitable. "I need some time to adjust to the idea," you might say, "but I will adjust because I love you and I want to be there for you."

Special note, however, for when it *is* actually about you, at least in that the person making the announcement is your spouse or partner. This involves a level of personal coping that is a bit beyond this book, and counseling is recommended. No two people will go through the same process. I like to believe that love is a powerful motivator toward equity – but on the other hand, a partnership must be fair to both members. If at all possible, seek guidance on dealing with this kind of change in a relationship.

Feel honored that you were told. The fact that they were willing to tell you means that you are important to them. Thank them for their trust in you.

Get clear instructions on how confidential you need to be about the situation. "Coming out" can be a very delicate matter, and your unexpected, unwarranted contributions won't help. Telling others is probably not your place. Ask your loved one questions about how you can best support them. This can include using their preferred name and pronouns, respecting their privacy, and advocating for their rights and well-being. "Do you want me to correct people who get your name or pronouns wrong?" If you don't know the answer, err on the side of caution and just keep quiet.

Don't question their decision. Remember that this is a deeply personal and thoughtful process, and they have likely given it thorough, serious and timely consideration. Trust their judgment and believe in their authenticity. By showing unwavering support and respect, you can play a significant role in fostering their self-confidence and well-being.

Remember that this person will remain the same person you care about. Your loved one is not vanishing to be replaced by a different human. People change throughout their lives. My friend Christina had a longtime friend who came out to her as gay; she says, "He'd been my friend for years. That was just the day I learned he'd been my gay friend for years."

Special note for transgender change: If your friend or loved one announces they are undergoing gender transition, the change may be a long and difficult process. Supporting someone who is undergoing gender transition is an essential aspect of creating a more inclusive and accepting society. When a loved one, friend, or colleague comes out as transgender, they are on a transformative journey.

Before delving into ways to support someone going through gender transition, it is essential to have a clear understanding of what that gender transition entails. Gender transition is a deeply personal process in which an individual aligns their gender identity with their true self. It involves various steps, such as changing one's name, pronouns, and presentation, seeking hormone therapy, and, in some cases, undergoing gender-affirming surgeries. It is a courageous journey that requires support and understanding from loved ones.

Respect and validate their identity. One of the most significant ways to support someone going through gender transition is by respecting and validating their identity. Affirming their gender identity is crucial in helping them feel seen, heard, and accepted. Ensure that you consistently use their preferred name and pronouns, even if it requires a period of adjustment. Mistakes may happen, but it is essential to apologize, correct yourself, and continue to honor their identity.

Celebrate milestones and progress. As someone's ally during their gender transition, it is important to celebrate their milestones and progress. Gender transitioning especially is a journey filled with significant moments, both big and small. Acknowledge and celebrate these milestones, whether it's legally changing their name, starting hormone therapy, or embracing their true self publicly.

CONCLUSION

Being an LGBTQ+ ally is an ongoing commitment to promoting equality, acceptance, and understanding. By educating yourself, taking action, and advocating for change, you can make a meaningful difference in the lives of LGBTQ+ individuals. Remember, allyship is a journey, so continue learning, growing, and challenging yourself to be the best ally you can be.

CHAPTER TWELVE:
FROM ALLYSHIP TO ACTIVISM

Never underestimate the power of allyship; if we were all allies to the LGBTQ+ community and women's rights, there would be no need for activism. Unfortunately, that is not the case yet, and so activism is a powerful tool for contributing to the fight for equality and acceptance. In this chapter, I'll describe some organizations (though it is by no means a complete listing!) which need our assistance. Our actions and generosity can make a real difference.

TAKING ACTION: HOW YOU CAN GET INVOLVED

You might be short on time, or unable to donate. That's okay! Remember, volunteering and donating are important, but there are many ways to support activism.

Volunteer: Many organizations rely on volunteers to carry out their important work. Consider volunteering your time and skills to support these organizations. Whether it's assisting with events, providing mentorship, or offering your expertise, your contribution can make a significant impact.

Donate: Financial contributions are vital for organizations to continue their work. Consider donating to support the programs and services they provide; even small donations can add up and make a difference.

Raise awareness: Use your voice to raise awareness about issues and the organizations that support these communities. Share information on social media, participate in campaigns and engage in conversations to promote understanding and acceptance.

Advocate: Support rights by advocating for inclusive policies and legislation. Attend rallies and protests and join advocacy campaigns to ensure rights are protected.

Write to your elected officials: Writing to an elected official may sound like a waste of time or a lot of trouble. We may believe politicians seldom listen to the words of ordinary citizens. But such messages can be remarkably effective. If an elected official gets one powerful letter from a constituent, they wisely understand that this opinion reflects that of *many* of their constituents.

You can find the correct emails and mailing addresses for your state senators at https://www.senate.gov/senators/senators-contact.htm, for your congresspersons at https://fiscalnote.com/find-your-legislator and for your representatives at https://www.house.gov/representatives.

Generally email is recommended for such messages, because letters take longer to arrive and are subject to extra layers of security clearance. Letters and emails to elected officials should follow these guidelines:

1. Be direct and specific. You do not have a lot of space to work with, so get to the point!

2. Limit your correspondence to one issue at a time.

3. State your issue or concern right away, in the email subject line or the first sentence of your letter.

4. Verify that you are indeed a constituent of this official's district; briefly add any personal connection that may exist, from voting for them, donating to their campaign, or attending their rallies or speeches. For example, "I am a resident of _______ District and was proud to contribute to your campaign and vote for you in 2022."

5. Personal stories are powerful. If possible, state how the issue directly impacts your life, or its "hometown relevance." The more meaningful you can make this, the more attention your message will get. Use anecdotal examples and "I" and "we" statements.

6. A general rule for persuasive messages is to stick with your three most important points. If you have research or facts that back up your points, add them briefly.

7. Don't make things up, attack individuals, or make threats or demands.

8. Frame your desire for support in a positive way and with courtesy, but be firm about your beliefs.

9. Thank the official for their time and attention.

10. Don't exceed one page for a letter or 500 words for an email.

AMPLIFYING LGBTQ+ VOICES

Advocacy organizations play a crucial role in promoting LGBTQ+ rights and ensuring that the community's voices are heard. These organizations work tirelessly to fight discrimination, challenge harmful policies, and create a more inclusive society. Here are a few notable advocacy organizations that can always use help.

The Human Rights Campaign (HRC)

The Human Rights Campaign is one of the largest LGBTQ+ advocacy organizations in the United States. Their mission is to ensure that LGBTQ+ individuals are treated equally and have the same rights and opportunities as everyone else. HRC works to pass pro-LGBTQ+ legislation, advocate for LGBTQ+ rights at the national level, and provide resources and support to the community. By supporting HRC, you can contribute to their efforts in creating a more inclusive society for all.

GLAAD

GLAAD is an organization dedicated to promoting LGBTQ+ representation and acceptance in the media. They work with media outlets, filmmakers, and content creators to ensure that LGBTQ+ stories are accurately and positively portrayed. GLAAD also provides resources and support to LGBTQ+ individuals and their families. By supporting GLAAD, you can help shape the narrative and increase visibility for the LGBTQ+ community.

The Trevor Project

The Trevor Project is a leading organization focused on preventing suicide among LGBTQ+ youth. They provide crisis intervention and suicide prevention services through their helpline, online chat, and text messaging platforms. The Trevor Project also offers resources and support to LGBTQ+ youth, their families, and educators. By supporting The Trevor Project, you can help save lives and provide much-needed support to vulnerable LGBTQ+ youth.

LGBTQ+ RESOURCES AND ASSISTANCE

Support organizations play a vital role in providing resources, assistance, and safe spaces for the LGBTQ+ community. They offer a range of services, from mental health support to community outreach programs. Here are a few such organizations that you can support.

LGBTQ+ Community Centers

LGBTQ+ community centers serve as hubs for the community, offering a wide range of services and programs. These centers provide a safe and welcoming space for LGBTQ+ individuals to connect, access resources, and receive support. They often offer counseling services, social activities, educational programs, and advocacy initiatives. By supporting your local LGBTQ+ community center, you can ensure that these essential services continue to be available to the community.

PFLAG

PFLAG (Parents, Families, and Friends of Lesbians and Gays) is an organization dedicated to supporting LGBTQ+ individuals and their families. They provide resources, education, and advocacy to promote understanding and acceptance within families and communities. PFLAG offers support groups, educational materials, and training programs to help families navigate the challenges of having an LGBTQ+ loved one. By supporting PFLAG, you can help create a more inclusive and accepting environment for LGBTQ+ individuals and their families.

LGBT Youth Organizations

LGBT youth organizations focus on providing support and resources specifically tailored to LGBTQ+ young people. These organizations offer safe spaces, mentorship programs, educational workshops, and counseling services to help LGBTQ+ youth navigate the challenges they face. By supporting LGBT youth organizations, you can provide vital support to young people who may be experiencing discrimination, bullying, or isolation.

LGBTQ+ Health Centers

LGBTQ+ health centers are dedicated to providing comprehensive healthcare services that are inclusive and affirming of LGBTQ+ individuals. These centers offer a range of services, including primary care, sexual health screenings, hormone therapy, and mental health support. By supporting LGBTQ+ health centers, you can help ensure that LGBTQ+ individuals have access to quality healthcare that respects their identities and specific healthcare needs.

LGBTQ+ Mental Health Organizations

Mental health organizations focused on the LGBTQ+ community work to address the unique mental health challenges faced by LGBTQ+ individuals. They offer counseling services, support groups, and resources to help LGBTQ+ individuals cope with issues such as coming out, discrimination, and mental health disorders. By supporting these organizations, you can contribute to the mental well-being of the LGBTQ+ community.

ACTIVISM FOR WOMEN'S RIGHTS

Over the past decade, women's rights have faced numerous challenges and setbacks across the globe. From the erosion of legal protections to the alarming increase in gender-based violence, the progress achieved in previous years has been threatened. The COVID-19 pandemic disproportionately affected women, particularly those working in the health sector, where 73.2% of employees are women. These women have faced extreme working conditions, longer work days, increased risk of contagion, and salary discrimination. The pandemic witnessed a steep increase in gender-based violence and further limitations on sexual and reproductive rights worldwide.

The fight for gender equality and women's empowerment is more important than ever. Luckily, there are organizations dedicated to supporting women's rights and working towards a more equitable future. These volunteer organizations provide opportunities for individuals to make a difference and contribute to the cause.

500 Women Scientists: Making Science Inclusive and Accessible

500 Women Scientists is a volunteer organization that aims to make science open, inclusive, and accessible. They fight against racism, patriarchy, and oppressive societal norms in the scientific community. Headquartered in Boulder, CO, their mission is to serve society by promoting gender equity in the field of science. Volunteers can support 500 Women Scientists by donating, joining their community, or partnering with them. Through these actions, individuals can contribute to creating a more equitable and inclusive scientific community.

Addressing Menstrual Health Inequality

Helping Women Period is just one of many volunteer organizations committed to supplying menstrual health products to homeless or low-income individuals. Their mission is to address the menstrual health inequality faced by vulnerable populations. Volunteers can contribute by making drawstring bags for discreet delivery, hosting menstrual health product drives, or purchasing merchandise. By supporting this and similar organizations, individuals can help ensure that menstruating individuals have access to the necessary products for their well-being.

<u>UN Women: Advancing Gender Equality Globally</u>

UN Women is a global organization that works towards advancing gender equality and women's empowerment worldwide. They run campaigns, professional networks, and initiatives to raise awareness, advocate for change, and provide support. Volunteers can get involved in various ways, such as subscribing to their newsletter, supporting their campaigns, joining their networks, or donating. By supporting UN Women, individuals can contribute to the global movement for gender equality and make a meaningful difference in the lives of women and girls.

<u>Equality Now: Protecting and Advancing Women's Rights</u>

Equality Now is an organization that uses the power of support to protect and advance women's rights. Their mission is to ensure every woman and girl can enjoy safety, choice, and respect. Volunteers can support Equality Now by making a gift, partnering with them, fundraising, or engaging in alternative ways of support. By getting involved, individuals can contribute to the fight for equality and help create a world where women and girls are treated with dignity and fairness.

ACTIVISM IN THE RIGHT-TO-CHOOSE MOVEMENT

In June 2022, the U.S. Supreme Court made a regressive decision by overturning the landmark ruling of Roe v. Wade, which had protected the right to abortion for over five decades. This decision dismantled the constitutional framework that safeguarded women's reproductive rights and returned the authority to regulate abortion to state legislatures.

Following the Supreme Court decision, a wave of abortion bans swept across the United States. As of January 2023, abortion has been banned in 14 states, severely limiting access to reproductive healthcare for millions of women. These bans vary in their scope, with some states imposing total prohibitions on abortion and others implementing restrictive regulations that make obtaining the procedure extremely challenging.

The consequences of the Supreme Court decision and state-level abortion bans have reverberated throughout the legal and policy systems. Women and girls across the country now face significant barriers in accessing comprehensive healthcare, including sexual and reproductive health services.

These bans not only restrict the right to abortion but also jeopardize numerous other human rights.

Right to Bodily Autonomy

Abortion bans infringe upon women's right to privacy and bodily autonomy, as recognized under international human rights law. The ability to make decisions about one's own body and reproductive choices is a fundamental aspect of personal freedom and self-determination.

Freedom of Expression and Thought

Women's reproductive choices are deeply personal and should be protected as forms of expression and thought. Abortion bans stifle women's freedom to make decisions about their own bodies and limit their ability to express their values and beliefs.

Freedom from Torture and Gender-Based Violence

Denying women access to safe and legal abortion can subject them to physical and psychological harm, constituting a form of torture and gender-based violence. Forced pregnancy and childbirth can result in severe physical and emotional trauma, violating women's rights to freedom from torture and cruel, inhuman, and degrading treatment.

The Disproportionate Impact on Marginalized Communities

Abortion bans have a disproportionate impact on women of color, who already face economic challenges and limited access to healthcare. These bans exacerbate existing economic disparities and perpetuate systemic inequalities.

Women with disabilities often face additional barriers in accessing healthcare, including reproductive services. Abortion bans can exacerbate these challenges by limiting their options and autonomy. These bans fail to consider the unique circumstances and medical needs of women with disabilities, denying them equal access to reproductive healthcare.

Low-income women, especially those living in rural areas, face significant obstacles in accessing abortion services due to geographical and financial constraints. Abortion bans further restrict their options and force them to travel long distances or seek unsafe alternatives. In states with abortion bans, there is a correlation with lower minimum wages and limited unionization levels. These economic policies compound the financial stress and economic insecurity faced by women. Lower wages and limited worker protections further exacerbate the economic disparities already experienced by marginalized communities, perpetuating inequality and hindering women's ability to access healthcare.

Erosion of Privacy Rights

Abortion bans contribute to a steady erosion of privacy rights, as law enforcement agencies and criminal investigators increasingly rely on data to track individuals seeking abortions or those who aid those women. Many states with abortion bans allow access to data related to abortion without a warrant. This unrestricted access undermines individuals' rights to privacy and creates an environment of surveillance and intrusion.

<u>Challenges Faced by Healthcare Professionals</u>

Abortion service providers across the country face an alarming increase in threats to their lives and safety. The hostile rhetoric surrounding abortion bans creates an environment of intimidation and violence. These threats not only endanger the lives of healthcare professionals but also contribute to the overall climate of fear and intimidation surrounding reproductive healthcare.

Healthcare professionals working in states with abortion bans often face risk management committees that determine the necessity of an abortion in urgent healthcare situations. These committees can hinder physicians' ability to provide the best medical care to their patients, jeopardizing their well-being. Additionally, healthcare professionals may face the risk of criminal prosecution for providing medically necessary or life-saving abortions.

Abortion bans and the restrictive environment surrounding reproductive healthcare create challenges in recruiting and retaining obstetricians and gynecologists. The hostile climate and potential legal consequences discourage healthcare professionals from practicing in states with abortion bans. This shortage of specialized medical professionals further limits women's access to essential reproductive healthcare services.

Even when physicians determine that an abortion is necessary, assembling a full healthcare team can be challenging due to the reluctance of other healthcare professionals. The hostile environment created by abortion bans can discourage medical professionals from participating in necessary procedures, making it difficult for physicians to provide comprehensive care.

While some states include exceptions in their abortion bans for cases where the mother's life is at risk or in instances of rape or incest, these exceptions often have limitations that do not align with medical diagnoses. The conditions for exceptions may be narrowly defined, excluding health-threatening situations.

UNDERSTANDING THE RIGHT-TO-CHOOSE MOVEMENT

The right-to-choose movement revolves around the belief that individuals should have the autonomy to make decisions about their reproductive health, including the choice to have an abortion. It recognizes that access to safe and legal abortion services is crucial for ensuring bodily autonomy, gender equality, and overall well-being. If you wish to show your support for the movement, here are just a few of the many organizations available.

The **Center for Reproductive Rights** stands as a global legal advocacy organization dedicated to advancing reproductive rights. Through landmark court victories, policy advocacy, and resources, they strive to protect and advance women's reproductive health, self-determination, and dignity as basic human rights. Their work spans a wide range of issues, including abortion, contraception, and maternal health, with a focus on strengthening reproductive health laws and policies globally.

Planned Parenthood is a well-known organization that offers a wide range of reproductive healthcare services, including abortion care. They provide vital support to individuals seeking information, education, and medical services related to sexual and reproductive health. Through their National Volunteer Program, volunteers have the opportunity to make a difference at both national and local levels, supporting Planned Parenthood's mission to ensure access to quality healthcare for all.

Unite for Reproductive & Gender Equity (URGE) is an organization focused on mobilizing young people to advocate for reproductive justice. Through their various programs and initiatives, they empower young activists to challenge oppressive systems and policies that limit reproductive freedom. By volunteering with URGE, individuals can support youth-led advocacy efforts and contribute to shaping a more inclusive and equitable future.

Volunteer organizations like **All Options** provide vital peer counseling and support services. These organizations offer unbiased counseling for pregnancy, parenting, adoption, and abortion, ensuring individuals have access to non-judgmental and compassionate guidance during challenging times. By volunteering as a peer counselor, you can directly assist individuals in navigating their reproductive choices and provide emotional support.

Political Engagement. Engaging in advocacy and political activism is another impactful way to support the right-to-choose movement. Organizations like the Planned Parenthood Action Fund offer opportunities to get involved in grassroots advocacy efforts, such as mobilizing voters, contacting legislators, and raising awareness about reproductive rights issues.

Volunteering at Clinics. Abortion clinics and funds rely on dedicated volunteers to provide critical support and ensure access to reproductive healthcare. Volunteers may assist with patient liaising, office administration, event coordination, and more. By contributing your time and skills, you directly contribute to the provision of safe and compassionate care for individuals seeking abortions.

CONCLUSION

Governments and international organizations must priori-tize the rights of women and girls, supporting and amplify-ing the voices of women human rights defenders and work-ing towards gender equality. It is essential to repeal regressive laws, provide essential services, promote equal access to edu-cation and employment, condemn gender-based violence, and protect women human rights defenders. No society can afford to tolerate the erosion of dignity for more than half its popu-lation.

♥

CHAPTER THIRTEEN:
ELUSIVE EQUITY

Gender equality has long been a goal for societies around the world, but progress has been slow and uneven. Despite significant advancements in women's education, economic participation, and political leadership, there are still many challenges to overcome in the pursuit of true equality. The question of equality is complicated by our changing understanding of gender. While true equity would mean ignoring gender altogether, human nature once more has tripped over its own ingrained habits. We imagine that gender equity somehow becomes a different issue if there are more than two genders involved, and a belief that is detrimental to all equity progress.

We have our work cut out for us over the next decade. As I conclude this book, let's take a look at the situation as it is now, and what we might see in the near future.

RECENT SETBACKS

COVID-19

One of the major setbacks to gender equality has been the COVID-19 pandemic. The global economic disruptions caused by the pandemic have disproportionately affected women, particularly those working in industries hit hard by the crisis, such as hospitality and service sectors. Women have been more likely to lose their jobs and have faced increased caregiving responsibilities, putting their careers and education on hold. Stay-at-home measures and social expectations have also put women at greater risk of domestic violence.

The economic recovery from the COVID-19 pandemic presents both opportunities and challenges for gender equality. Developed economies are expected to recover faster, while emerging markets and developing countries may take longer to rebound. Studies of previous recessions indicate that women have more difficulty regaining employment and recouping lost wages during recovery. Regional variations in economic recovery will affect women's ability to reenter the workforce in different countries.

Slowing progress

In recent years, progress towards gender equality has also slowed in some areas. While there have been significant improvements in women's education, there are still challenges in expanding access to secondary education. Basic levels of education have largely been achieved, but higher-level goals are more difficult to reach. Additionally, the persistence of patriarchal attitudes in many regions has hindered further progress.

In many parts of the world, women have limited or no rights to land ownership, even in countries where laws allow for it. This lack of access to land and property can hinder women's economic empowerment and limit their opportunities for advancement.

Despite improvements in women's labor force participation, there are still significant disparities in paid labor and wage equality. Women are more likely to work in the informal sector, have limited opportunities for entrepreneurship, and are underrepresented in STEM fields. Women also face challenges in accessing leadership positions and political participation, with only about 25% of legislators worldwide being women.

<u>Violence and devaluation</u>

Violence against women remains a significant challenge to gender equality. Sexual violence, including domestic and partner violence, continues to be a global issue. The WHO estimates that more than one in four women have experienced physical or sexual violence from an intimate partner in their lifetime. Violence against women not only affects their physical and mental well-being but also reduces economic productivity.

Skewed sex ratios, resulting from sex-selected abortion and killings of newborn baby girls, are a manifestation of the devaluation of women in some societies. Child brides, prevalent in parts of Sub-Saharan Africa and South Asia, face limited access to education and economic opportunities, as well as higher risks of domestic violence and maternal injury.

<u>Healthcare and legal protections withheld</u>

LGBTQ+ individuals still face numerous challenges in their daily lives. Discrimination, misgendering, and limited access to healthcare and legal protections are among the key obstacles they encounter. LGBTQ+ individuals often have to navigate situations where they must decide whether or not to disclose their gender identity, considering their safety, comfort, and the necessity of others knowing.

Access to appropriate healthcare is crucial for LGBTQ+ individuals. Many LGBTQ+ individuals seek medical interventions, such as hormone therapy or gender-affirming surgeries, as part of their gender transition. Ensuring that healthcare providers are knowledgeable and sensitive to the unique needs of LGBTQ+ individuals is essential for promoting their overall well-being.

LGBTQ+ individuals often face legal challenges due to the lack of recognition and protection for their gender identity.

Legal frameworks should be updated to include LGBTQ+ individuals, ensuring their rights and protections in areas such as identification documents, employment, and public services. Gender-neutral language should be adopted to ensure inclusivity and respect for all gender identities.

WHAT CAN BE DONE

To achieve equity, concerted efforts are needed at various levels, including societal, legal, and educational spheres. We must challenge existing norms, promote awareness and understanding, and advocate for policy changes that offer opportunities to, and protect the rights and well-being of, all individuals.

Break Barriers in the Workplace

Promoting gender equality in the workplace is essential for closing the gender gap. Addressing wage disparities, increasing diverse representation in leadership positions, and supporting entrepreneurship are key steps toward achieving equality. Companies and organizations can implement policies and practices that promote diversity and inclusion, ensuring equal opportunities for everyone to thrive professionally.

Increase Education and Awareness

Educational institutions play a vital role in promoting understanding and acceptance of an inclusive world. Incorporating inclusive curricula that cover gender diversity and LGBTQ+ experiences can help foster a more inclusive and empathetic society. It is also essential to provide training and resources for educators to support LGBTQ+ students effectively.

<u>Policy Changes and Legal Protections</u>

Advocacy for legal changes and protections is crucial for advancing LGBTQ+ equity and protecting women's reproductive rights. LGBTQ+ individuals should have the legal right to update their identification documents to reflect their gender identity accurately. Legislation should also be enacted to prohibit discrimination based on gender identity and ensure equal rights and opportunities for LGBTQ+ individuals in all areas of life.

<u>Community Support and Allyship</u>

Building a supportive community is vital for equity. Allies play a crucial role in challenging discrimination, advocating for rights, and creating safe spaces for individuals to express themselves.

LOOKING TOWARDS EQUITY

While there are significant challenges to overcome, the growing visibility and recognition of humanity's expansive variety offers hope for a more inclusive future. The younger generation, in particular, has shown greater acceptance and understanding of gender diversity. Continued efforts to challenge societal norms, promote education and awareness, and advocate for legal protections will contribute to achieving equity in the next ten years and beyond.

Before closing, I'd like to revisit a quote from anchorperson Nydia Han, who encompassed the most basic level of equity that we can practice on a daily basis.

"Unfamiliarity breeds fear and fear breeds hate. We have to approach each other with curiosity to find understanding and love."

If we all engage in that simple practice, equity won't have to be decreed by a government or from a boardroom. We can build it from the ground up.

ABOUT ATMOSPHERE PRESS

Founded in 2015, Atmosphere Press was built on the principles of Honesty, Transparency, Professionalism, Kindness, and Making Your Book Awesome. As an ethical and author-friendly hybrid press, we stay true to that founding mission today.

If you're a reader, enter our giveaway for a free book here:

SCAN TO ENTER
BOOK GIVEAWAY

If you're a writer, submit your manuscript for consideration here:

SCAN TO SUBMIT
MANUSCRIPT

And always feel free to visit Atmosphere Press and our authors online at atmospherepress.com. See you there soon!

♥

ABOUT THE AUTHOR

ALEXANDRA MCGROARTY is a Certified Diversity Professional and Human Resources Consultant based out of South Jersey. She has previous corporate and consulting experience building diversity, equity, inclusion strategies for businesses and associations as well as implementing diversity initiatives across various levels of the employee lifecycle. She has also given several talks on the importance of gender equity in schooling and the workplace.

Alex previously published *Bridging the Gap: Reducing Gender Bias in the Workforce* in 2022 and two works in the grief space: *So Now What, Harnessing Grief after Life's Major Losses* and *Until We Meet Again, Leo* in 2023.

In her free time, Alex likes to travel and spend time with her family and children, Lucas and Ava.

www.ingramcontent.com/pod-product-compliance
Lightning Source LLC
Chambersburg PA
CBHW021538150726
47990CB00006B/2304